THE

OTHER SIDE

OF

HOPE

*Flipping the Script on Cynicism and Despair
and Rediscovering Our Humanity*

Danielle Strickland

W PUBLISHING GROUP

AN IMPRINT OF THOMAS NELSON

THE OTHER SIDE OF HOPE:

Theory

CONTENTS

PREFACE

I once visited an art gallery on the southern cape of South Africa. My friend and I took our time traveling the coastline, visiting towns and exploring the glorious landscape—rolling vineyards, majestic sea views, and the rich red earth of KwaZulu-Natal. My friend had selected art galleries she really wanted to visit along the route. So on one beautiful day we made our way to one. What we found when we arrived would annoy her and amaze me. The exhibit for the week was called *The Flip Side* and consisted of every single piece of art in the entire gallery being flipped over. The displays were simply the backsides of what I'm assuming were amazing works of art. What we saw was not glorious colors or expert shadowing or lifelike drawings of people, no ships or crosses or landscapes—only wood and nails and beige paper and some wire that allowed the pictures to hang. We saw the part no one is supposed to see. The part that has its back up against the wall—and for good reason I suppose. It was the rugged bits—some with little names marked on them, some with rips and tears, but most just remarkably ordinary. No matter how incredible the artist was or how remarkably original the work might be, the other side of the painting was, well, normal. Earthy. Maybe it isn't what we drove several hours to see—but I'll never forget it.

Something deep was deposited in my soul that day. It caused me to stop and think about the other side of my life. Not the front-facing glorious thing I was painting but the nails and wood that held it together—the beige paper that lined my life. The hook I hung my life from. If I were to flip my life around, what would others see?

The other side.

So when I'm talking about the other side of hope, I find myself back in the art gallery. I want to talk about the side of hope that doesn't look glorious or fabulous and doesn't really fit on the front of a greeting card. I want to talk about the side of hope we must hammer together and line our lives with—if any of what we are wanting to live can be seen. I want to talk about the "unsexy" side of hope—where we leave the slogans aside and just tell the truth and discover the truth for ourselves and our world. Sometimes that hope is hard to make sense of, especially since truth is multifaceted. What I mean is, hope, like its siblings faith and love, is difficult to nail down. But we are in deep need of figuring out how to find some. So, with a nod to the art curator in that obscure gallery on the other side of the world, I'm framing a theory of hope, identifying the enemies of hope and how to fight them. And then flipping this book over, I'll paint some stories of where hope has been present, absent, elusive, and transformative in my own experience. The story side is not obvious, because art is meant to raise questions, not answer them. But the stories are beautiful and provocative.

I'm painting ones that reveal more of my own story than I ever have before. When I talk to my artist friends, they say every art piece is an exposing of their inner self, and to display them is an incredibly vulnerable act. That's how I feel with these stories. The theory side is like wood nailed together—it's rough and not very shiny, but it holds. And that's all we really need hope to do.

one

ILLUSIVE HOPE

I'm scared about this book.

Hope is so overdone. And by *overdone* I don't just mean the title and the concept and the use of it everywhere from shampoo products to political-campaign slogans to cosmetic surgery. Advertisements even suggest hope is connected to the fleshy fat cells on my upper thighs. No, I mean it's overcooked. It's oversold. What was supposed to be fleshy and tender and juicy has been submitted to our panic about it being not quite cooked enough. Like hope is a piece of chicken on a barbecue. So we've overcooked it, and while it's technically meat, it's really tough to chew and dry as sandpaper. We've overcooked it by saying the same things over and over again, almost believing that if we say them enough, hope will manifest through our cadence. Like we are working up a frenzy of emotional survival and thinking it might catch on. But hope, real hope, is uncontrollable, unpredictable, and most often unexpected.

Maybe the trouble with hope is that it's spontaneous and not performative. Like my kids at their cutest stages. So adorably cute but never, ever on demand. On demand they turned into shy or cantankerous little people, refusing to show their faces or smile on cue, accompanied by my apologies or awkward jokes to assure all onlookers that they are normally so cute and gregarious. When my eldest son was a toddler, he would only roar at people. I'm serious. Like, even really *important* people. And he was such a cute kid. People would come near him and look at him in his beautiful blue eyes and smile and say, "Ah, look at you, beautiful baby!" and he would open his eyes and mouth and as loud as he could he would deliver a roar. And not with a cute, smiling face, like "What a cute little lion you are" kind of roar. Nope. A genuine loud and scary roar with wide eyes and a serious face, and it would *scare* people.

They would take a step back and open their wide eyes and glance at me with a quizzical look because they didn't know what to do. And what did they want me to do? What should I tell them? That he doesn't normally roar all the time? That he's really a nice little kid when no one is looking at him? I mean, those things are all true, but what good would it do? He even did it to Eva Burrows, the former world leader of the Salvation Army. The Mother Teresa of the movement called to serve the poor. Her elderly, gracious frame bent over to have a proper look at this gorgeous baby boy, and that perfect round-faced cherub launched a lion's roar and promptly swatted her face. That kid would never perform. What was so common and normal in daily places was nearly impossible to demand when everyone was looking. And isn't that a little like hope?

Maybe hope is a crazy-cute child who refuses to perform when we demand her to.

I've had a hunch over the past many years that hope is wild

and fleshy and raw, spontaneous and bubbling over, uncontrollable at any moment, anywhere, anytime.

And when it appears, it is best to go for the ride.

One time at a Christian event I was on a panel and we were discussing very important things—and then we got the giggles. I mean, we got the kind of giggles that summon the evil eye of your parents and then finally get you escorted out of church altogether because, try as you might, you just can't control what's happening to you. And the more you try to hold in the giggles the more awkward and loud your gurgling brook of comedy gets until it becomes a virtual river of uncontrollable laughter. And that's exactly what happened. There wasn't much of a stink eye, or any escorts out of the building, because we were all in it together. I mean, who is going to physically remove the entire leadership panel from the platform of a conference? We all lost it. And then everyone else lost it too. And we just laughed and laughed and laughed for the entire session when we were supposed to be talking about important things that everyone had paid to come and hear. And it was glorious. The holiest thing I've been at. What were we laughing at? I don't even know. We just lost it. Lost control. Lost the capacity to pretend like we knew what we were talking about. Maybe it was just existential angst at the sheer meaningless of everything. Emotional exhaustion in the midst of a hard schedule. It wasn't the usual culprits—we were alcohol-free, and cannabis still wasn't a normal thing yet. Maybe it was God? The holy rollers among us sure thought so. It was a sovereign thing. God struck us with holy laughter. I wondered if there was a different kind of laughter. After all, Anne Lamott is mostly always right and she told us that "laughter is carbonated holiness."[1] The strangest thing about it was what happened when it was over. None of us were sad or embarrassed or even apologetic. We were filled with a bubbling joy, and deep in my weary bones I felt hope. Hope that there is something much larger than my controllable behavior or leadership ability. Hope that God does indeed work in mysterious and often comical ways.

But hope is also elusive and hidden. It can seem to disappear when we need it, or when we want it to perform, or even when we just need its assurance that we aren't alone or totally lost in this world that's on fire. Hope's absence is so noticeable and scary that it forces us to conjure it up and say stupid things that we read on a poster or that someone really happy told us. So we just keep saying things that sound right but feel wrong. We will our words to catch something real so we can use them to drag ourselves out of the pit of despair we feel ourselves falling into. I've done this.

I have so many friends who struggle with depression—one who spends her days willing herself to stay alive. Every day she fights to hang on. To hold on. To get through the darkness. To keep treading water in what seems like an endless ocean of despair. And what do I say to her? Usually really dumb-sounding things that ring so hollow, that are so insufficient—"Hold on to hope" or "You've got this"—and even as it comes out of my mouth I wince at the inadequacy of it. There is hope refusing to perform again.

EXODUS

The way we so often do "hope" these days reminds me of that story in Exodus when God's people were waiting for Moses to return from the mountaintop and were running out of patience for some kind of news about where they were going or what they were going to do now that they were free and stuck in the desert with no promised land in sight and their leader gone. Surely after an entire month of waiting for his return from a mountaintop—covered with darkness, flashing with lightning, and rolling with thunder—even the most hopeful among them began to panic. He was never coming back. And they needed something. Like, now. Something to hang on to. Something to bring them some kind of solace. Some kind of distraction. Some kind of evidence of connection and transcendence. Some kind of meaning or—hope. Right. Hope. You can probably feel it. The panic. The underlying truth of their helpless predicament slowly dawning on them. The adults speaking in whispers to protect the children from their inevitable demise in the desert with no leader in sight. Forty days. That's how long Moses was gone. By himself. Without food or water. Out of sight. Forty days.

Most preachers I've heard tend to be pretty hard on the Israelites. Even Moses wasn't happy. He lost it. When he returned all excited with the news of a way of life and the presence of God and their calling as a people, he came at the exact wrong time. The frenzy had already started. The need for something to hang on to was already in full swing. If you can't find an ethereal eternal being to show up on demand, you can always make something shiny. That's what they did.

They threw all the gold they had together, melted it, and made their own god—a statue of Baal—a god they knew how to make. A god they met in Egypt. A visible god. A shiny one.

Shiny: a value they could calculate. A god they could touch and see. In our search for hope, the gods we make are much

5

the same as a shiny golden calf. Trinkets of epic proportions, evidence of our attempts to control and manipulate hope.

THE FIGHT FOR HOPE

The fight for hope in the midst of despairing times is fraught with danger. We instinctively reach out for something to hang on to. Anything really. Carbs or guns, cannabis or sex—even Amazon. What are we looking for? Some measure of defense, small promises or miserable friends that make us feel more in control for a moment or two. Gods we can make. This is a tale as old as time. I want a god—but in my own image. I want a god who can perform just the way I'd like when the cameras are on, when the people are watching. And it works. For a while. For a short while the god I make actually brings me comfort. A small relief from despair. Relief enough to lift the burden of dread. But what those gods can't give us is genuine hope. Distraction, yes. Momentary company, yes. Dopamine, in small bursts, for sure. Friendship, of a kind. Many of my friends who struggled with addiction refer to their drug of choice as a bad friend. But still a friend. And when loneliness is the pit of your own despair, then any friend is better than none.

That's why I'm nervous about this book.

A book on hope. What was I thinking?

I don't have any slogans for you to memorize or trinkets for you to melt and fashion into a god who shows up at the time you need it. Nope. I don't even have the right things to say to my own friends who are in the pit of despair. I don't have Hallmark-movie moments either, where miraculous hope enters the scene and everyone lives happily ever after. In fact, I know a lot of Cinderellas who hold on to slippers that still don't fit. But I'll tell you what I do have.

I have this sneaking suspicion and personal experience that if we would stop trying so hard to manufacture it, if we could refuse to put hope into a perfect answer or beautiful slogan, if we could simply let go and relax into God, who is at work in this world whether we can see it clearly or not, hope might just appear.

I have a friend who is a hunter. Well, to be more honest, he goes hunting. The thing is, he never returns with anything. I asked him one year after his annual trip why he didn't shoot anything. "What happens in the woods?" I mean, is he just a terrible hunter? And he told me about the first time he saw a deer. He was just a teenager and doing the annual pilgrimage with his father. He was learning to be a man. "My dad told me I had to lie very still and be very patient and if we waited long enough and were quiet enough, we might find ourselves a deer." On this occasion, he saw not just a deer but a mother deer and her fawn. "It was the most beautiful, peaceful, and glorious sight I had ever seen. I held my breath with wonder as I watched these incredible animals together. It felt so sacred and so joyful." He went on, "I heard my father breathe out slowly as he pulled the trigger, just like he had taught me to do. And I watched this majestic and beautiful animal in front of me go down with one shot. He had killed the mother, and I started to cry. My father was exuberant at the kill and exasperated by my blubbering. He told me to 'man up.' But I could not shake the sadness. He had killed something beautiful. And no matter how many times I go hunting, when I see a deer, I can never shoot it. I simply behold it. And the joy I feel is hard to explain. You see, I found many deer this year. But I don't shoot them. I see them and celebrate their beauty."

I was genuinely shocked. And moved. This man had all the appearances of someone who loves hunting. He has all the tools and clothes and attitude. But underneath all that camouflaged manly facade was a boy trying to find some beauty. In a way I feel like he captured the other side of hunting for hope. Its illusive nature is something we want to capture. To put on our mantels. To hang the horns of hope on our lives as victors of despair. But maybe the greater calling, the bigger task, is to behold hope, to allow hope to invite us into a new way of being, seeing, living in the world. Maybe the illusive quality of hope is a gift to behold, not a conquered thing to possess.

I have an undaunted trust that God is going to show up. I'm utterly convinced that hope springs up at the most unlikely of times and is worth waiting for. I think I finally understand that the fear crouching at our doors might not be as final or scary as we think. That the real power to hang on to when things are tough is found in waiting for a person, not a trick. And that finding hope might require going deeper in, not getting out of our nagging sense of unworthiness. Actually, the hope I have has required me to take off a heavy external pressure and uncover and expose a deeply rooted dread. It turns out hope, when it's ready—or maybe when we are ready—can liberate us from our false illusions of what hope is supposed to look like. So, with that kind of hope in mind, let's flip everything over and behold the other side.

two

CYNICISM AND DESPAIR:
The Twin Enemies

When I told my friend I was writing a book about how to push back against cynicism, she laughed. And it wasn't a holy laughter. She was laughing at me. Apparently I'm cynical. Maybe it's the time I've spent in hard neighborhoods steeling my heart from getting broken with the steady pace of bad news. Possibly it's the many times I've been left to deal with the fallout of bad leadership. Or maybe, just maybe, it's the embarrassing, seemingly endless times I've assumed the best of people (and systems) and was left disappointed and feeling pretty dumb. It could just be that I've watched too much TV. What I do know for sure is that I don't *want* to be cynical. I definitely don't want to land in the pit of despair (yes, I'm using a *Princess Bride* reference). I do know that I struggle with assuming the worst of other people's motivations (which is cynicism). And I also know that if I allow cynicism to lead me, it takes me down into dark places. I don't want to live in the dark. What I understand as I've researched for this book is that I'm not alone. Not by a long shot. Cynicism and despair tower over our dreaming capacity like mountains blocking out the sun. These twin giants of our time threaten to keep us all in the dark and paralyzed by fear.

Sociologists say we are in a mental health crisis. And they keep saying this. Every year it worsens. And it is the same with addiction. During the COVID-19 crisis mental health hotlines increased their intake by over 700 percent.[1] The ongoing public health crisis of opioid overdoses and suicide rages on.[2] Have you felt the impact of this in your own life? Maybe you've been there. Maybe it's your own life you've been hanging on to by a thread—or maybe you've been trying to help others find hope in these trying times. It's tough. So many of my friends have suffered with growing addictions, and finding them help (especially affordable help) has been a gutting experience. Treatment centers are hard to find, and waiting lists keep people struggling to hang on. People are lost and suffering in ways we cannot fully fathom. We can feel the effects, but what is happening? A group of doctors asked this same question. Alarmed by rising premature mortality from suicides, drug poisoning, and alcoholic liver disease, the group clarified the term used to describe this phenomenon—"deaths of despair"—and sought to explore the implications.[3]

DESPAIR

The simple definition of despair is "the absence of hope."[4] But as this group of doctors suggests, the way despair works can be much more complicated and the implications far reaching. They cite the work on depression in individuals that highlighted despair manifesting not only in the mind but in emotions, behaviors, and biology. But they say it's deeper and wider than just an individual malady. "Despair can arise in, spread through, and affect social contexts, including social networks and communities."[5]

I think they are spot on. I sense the despair in our culture, in generations. Can you? Kids are glued to their phones, scared to make real contact with real people. Husbands and wives go out for dinner with nothing but bad news to commiserate about. I've had a thousand small conversations about things that will never change. People lament about the world being at its worst, which is measurably not true but doesn't really matter because despair doesn't really care about the facts. Despair is connected to how we feel. It's as though despair has manifested itself in the air we breathe, the news we watch, the conversations we have with our families and friends. The loss of hope is palpable. Resigning to the overwhelming sense that we can't change anything is sold as a relief. In conversations I've been having with a vast range of people, from pastors to teachers to students to children, despair is threatening not only our lives; it's threatening our communities. In their study on despair, experts suggest that despair has four domains. Let's look at them. If we want to fight back against despair, it'll be helpful to understand what we are up against.

- **Cognitive despair:** "Thoughts indicating defeat, hopelessness, guilt, worthlessness, learned helplessness, pessimism, and limited positive expectations for the future." Someone suffering this kind of despair has a bias that assumes an antagonistic attitude about others (interpreting others' actions as against them).

- **Emotional despair:** "Includes feelings of excessive sadness, irritability, hostility, loneliness, anhedonia, and apathy." A feature of this domain is irritability and interpersonal conflict. Relationships are difficult.

- **Behavioral despair:** "Risky, reckless, and unhealthy acts that are self-destructive and reflect limited consideration of the future (e.g., high-risk sexual behaviors, gambling, self-harm, reckless driving, excessive spending, criminal activity, smoking, substance use, low physical activity)." This includes those using coping behaviors to combat despair or despairing behaviors because it doesn't really matter. The behaviors are often the same, regardless of the motive.

- **Biological despair:** "Occurs when the body's stress-reactive systems no longer function homeostatically and show signs of dysregulation or depletion, which constitutes a biological correlation of, and sometimes a basis for, cognitive, emotional, and behavioral despair." Simply put, this means you physically cannot change your mood or alter your hormones or regulate your stress levels. Your body can manifest despair through its own shutdown or malfunction.[6]

This overview of despair is intense. But it's even more complicated than just a personal battle. The introduction of social despair is what is most mind-blowing about the new research. Mental health experts have primarily studied people's individual journeys with despair. But the collective, social aspects of despair felt in culture and generations by whole groups of people is also worthy of consideration. The collective experience of trauma can be a trigger to widespread despair in groups.

I interviewed Sami Awad, a Palestinian peace activist, on a recent podcast episode and asked him about the current state of affairs in Israel/Palestine.[7] His answer was fascinating. He believes that the issue at the heart of the conflict is based in collective trauma. He wholeheartedly believes that without collective efforts to identify and deal with the trauma faced by both Jews and Arabs there will be no peace in the Middle East. Peace talks are always about behavior, land, economy—which are all externally based. But the way we think and feel about those decisions is as important as the details of the decisions themselves. The despair of peace talks in the Middle East is more connected to emotional hopelessness rooted in trauma than in any division of land or resources. Fascinating.

Think about this in our own context. I had a conversation with a friend about her guilt for feeling hopeless. "How can I be depressed? My life is totally fine. I have everything I need. What is wrong with me?" The problem with despair is that it's not always about the external facts. Despair manifests internally. What's fascinating is how this internal malady can manifest in any culture. Yet even though despair can be an internal reality threatening anyone, recent collective-despair studies are revealing that despair can spread through whole communities because of external factors as well.

Economic hardship in regions or in people groups can also lead to despair. Consider trying to survive the winter in Afghanistan with no governmental support, or access to your money (banks are closed), or even foreign help (economic sanctions and embargos). What about your children's future without education or enough food? Exposure to adversity and struggle without relief or success can also be a despair spreader. I've walked with many Indigenous women suffering the realities of systemic oppression. The collective grief and trauma that seems to never end—death, addiction, oppression, sexual abuse, and a government and people bent on rejecting and dismissing you—is a recipe for social despair.

Powerful emotional responses to events can spread through social networks. Regular comparisons on social media tend to "spread despair" in connected groups. It turns out despair is not just something happening inside of us. Though it starts inside, it works its way outward, becoming an infectious disease. In other words, you can catch despair.

I've got a hunch that one of the things that spreads despair is its twin: cynicism. Cynicism is the loss of hope in others. It's an inclination to believe that people are motivated purely by self-interest. Despair is a loss of hope in general, but cynicism fuels us toward its destructive power. Our cynical disappointment with others (near and far) cultivates and accelerates the disease of despair.

Cynicism and despair both have complex strategies that entrench and define our perspectives and actions. Both live in the shadows of our lives and remain almost invisible until we suddenly, and often surprisingly, catch a glimpse of their ugly faces in our day-to-day work. We can hear their deadening voices in our own thoughts. Have you ever heard something genuinely terrible and shrugged your shoulders and said, "That's life"? It feels like one day we wake up and start agreeing with the dominant despairing view of the world, shrinking into the shape of its seemingly meaningless rhythms. I remember reading a book called *The End of Hunger*. The general idea is usually grasped by the title but it took me a few chapters. Somewhere around chapter 3 I started to genuinely grasp that it might be possible to end extreme global hunger. That's called hope. And as soon as I had that hopeful thought, I realized that I had believed—for my whole life—that hunger was inevitable. Something we just had to live with. I had been living with a despairing attitude about extreme hunger. And that despair was shared. It was no wonder hardly anyone was committing to take real action against the global hunger crisis—we were in despair and cynical about anyone who thought otherwise. Agreeing—if not explicitly, then implicitly—with the idea that nothing we do really matters is despair. Believing that change, if not impossible, is too hard and that what little we offer is not enough is despair. Believing everyone else thinks that, too, is cynicism.

I don't know what happens to you when you feel despair seeping into your thoughts and heart, but I feel *shame*. This is the complicated nature of cynicism and despair. I know I shouldn't feel hopeless or jaded, but I still do. That's why I was captivated by another study that explored (in areas suffering from conflict) why spreading despair is easier, and more effective, than spreading hope. They gleaned from their research that messages of hope and despair have different effects on people based on their underlying attitudes regarding the conflict, or in other words, their political ideology.[8] Our values, attitudes, and perceptions directly affect how we feel and what we do with hope or despair. The study discovered that people who are most set in their prescribed future (political worldview, expectations, desired outcomes) become the most hopeless during periods of uncertainty. Whoa. I think I need to write that again. The more set you are on your idealized future, the more susceptible to cynicism and despair you are during times of uncertainty. Do you remember when I introduced hope as wild and fluid? Well, it turns out that despair is rooted in certainty. In other words, when you have a prescribed idea of what hope will look like—"The only hope for my country is if X is in leadership," or "The only hope for my future is if I find a partner," or "There is no hope for my business without a massive change in the economy." Whatever your certainty looks like is where despair can take root. It boils down to this: the more rigid we are, the more despairing we become—and not just in our thoughts but also in our actions.

Well, that little dive into despair probably didn't make you feel hopeful. But here is the thing: the other side of hope can't be found until we face the realities of despair.

Now that I know despair can affect every part of my life (mind, will, emotions, body) and actually affects and infects the people around me (social connections / group despair), so what? Does this make anything better?

Maybe we can't solve every far-reaching implication of despair in the world, but it does help us begin. And like with every social malady, there is a moment when it becomes quite obvious that the fight begins with me. I pray that moment is now.

Note: I want to pause here to say that depression is a real disease that has life-threatening implications. If you are suffering from despair in a personally profound and debilitating way, please get help from a doctor. The cultural despair that is existential angst and blankets our collective thoughts and actions is important, but before you dive into that in the rest of the book, please consider getting help from a professional right now.

three

UNDER THE
FLOORBOARDS

On the door of my fridge is a magnet someone bought me that reads, "Eat and drink today for tomorrow we diet." I feel like it could be a motto for my life.

Perhaps it's despair that fuels the Epicurean philosophy that tells us to eat, drink, and be merry, for tomorrow we die. Isn't that just hopelessness turned outward? We shrug off change, even in our own life, because nothing we do seems to matter. What is sold as "freedom" to do whatever we like no matter what the consequences is actually despair driving us to do nothing. I was talking with a twenty-one-year-old about voting during a recent election. She wasn't going to bother voting because she believed it wouldn't matter anyway. She's not alone. Her feelings are despair turned outward. It's not the inward despair that says she doesn't matter. It's the outward despair that says what she does won't matter.

It's a tricky adversary, though, because it doesn't feel like despair on my first trip to the kitchen to eat the brownie—it feels like hope. But by my third trip, fifteen minutes later, I'm despairing. Am I alone? Despair causes some of us to turn inward and hide—ashamed of the looming hopeless thoughts that simmer at our core—turning up other voices to drown out their mocking tone. "I'm fine," we squeak out when people ask. "I've got so much to be thankful for." We scold ourselves for our lack of joy and stick up a pithy Bible verse on our mirrors. But it ends up mocking us instead of helping us, because, ultimately, we haven't squared off with an enemy—we haven't confronted the problem—and the seething pit of this invisible threat is crouching at the door of our hearts and minds, ready to pounce. And the truth is, we cannot defeat what we will not confront.

I was only twenty-nine years old and fully immersed in an urban ministry. We had moved into the community with high hopes for transformation and loads of personal affirmation and spiritual confirmation about being in the right place at the right time. We even had quite a bit of early success. But a lot of my friends died. People die in that neighborhood a lot. Carved into the heart of Canada's "best city to live in" is the Downtown Eastside. Eight blocks, seven thousand drug addicts. Drug addiction, a mental health crisis, general lack of access to good food, and years of hard living kills people.

I had just discovered that my friend had been found dead in her small, dingy room in a slum rooming house, all by herself for what looked like many days, most likely over a week. No one had even noticed her gone for over a week. Not even me. And I hit rock bottom. It was grief for sure. Grief over losing her, but also a deep grief over the life she had lost years before her physical body gave out. Grief that she was all alone when we had talked so much about community. Grief that we didn't even find her. Grief that she was one of many who had died recently and I was out of grief. The wave of hopelessness at the reality of what we were facing overwhelmed me. And I wept. For quite a while—a lot longer than normal.

In the middle of this weeping my mother called to see how I was. I managed to control the conversation fairly well, sounding upbeat and happy in order to keep my mother shielded from the darkness in my mind and heart. "I'm fine," I choked out. But my mother knows all about the dark battle of trying to hang on to hope in the midst of an overwhelming defeat. So she stuck with her questioning. "You don't sound like yourself. Is everything really okay? What's happening, hon?" And eventually I couldn't respond. I could only weep. "What are you so sad about, Dani?" she asked and then just waited. And surprisingly I answered her—perhaps the most honest I have ever answered before.

"I feel like my life doesn't matter. Like nothing I do matters. I don't matter."

And the sobs came in wave after wave after wave. And my mother just sat with me in the dark. The waves slowly passed but the thought remained, lodged like a sliver in my mind. And this is what I mean about the other side of hope. Because lodged in these reflections, these honest and naked questions, are important implications that if faced, instead of avoided, might unlock real, authentic hope. Does my life even matter? This can be a despairing question, or if I'm brave enough to follow it all the way through, it could also be a hopeful one. And this is what's hard about the other side of hope. What we want hope to do is rescue us from our deep, dark thoughts and the inner turmoil of our lives. But authentic hope requires us to go through them and come out the other side. Hope isn't scared of the dark. What gives my life meaning? Why am I here? Those are the questions we must answer, not avoid, if hope is going to be real.

There is no harm in understanding the brevity of life and the fragility of our human predicament—but if we stay there, without a friend, we can get lost. Hope is a friend who leads us through the dark.

Years after that conversation with my mom, I stood on a stage in front of thousands of teenagers with a message about their worthiness and God's intention to bring life to the full. As I was speaking, I had an overwhelming sense of urgency. When I was finished, my friend Mike Pilovachi (the host of the event) came to the stage and we had a quick chat about what we were both sensing. I felt led to ask a very direct question around those struggling with suicidal thoughts and self-harm. Mike agreed.

Stepping back to the microphone, with Mike at my side, I queried, "Is anyone struggling with suicidal thoughts or thoughts of self-harm today?"

I knew that this was a big swing. I was nervous as I looked into a sea of faces.

I continued, "God sees you. If this is you, I want to invite you to stand up so that we can pray with you."

No one stood. There was a palpable nervous energy in the arena.

I kept sharing, "The people around you are going to pray with me, because we want to surround you with love as we choose life together."

As I spoke these words, students began to stand.

I didn't know if it was the right thing to do, but I did sense an urgency to do something—so that's what I did. I was expecting a few dozen brave people to stand. Instead, two-thirds of the room stood up. Thousands and thousands (the event held nine thousand) of teenagers stood because they had contemplated suicide or were dealing with self-harm. The collective confession of a generation took our breaths away.

I remember Mike and me instinctively taking a step backward on the stage, overwhelmed with what we were dealing with. There was weeping, crying, and even screaming. It was intense. And scary. And also incredibly hopeful. It was hopeful because the darkness had been exposed. Those kids had the courage to square off with their despair. To tell on it.

Whatever lives in the dark festers and grows, keeping us afraid and stuck. But God isn't afraid of the dark. Don't get me wrong here. I'm not saying those thousands of kids were instantly healed of depression because of a public prayer time. Hope isn't magic. But exposing the despair to the light allowed hope to get in. And hope leads us through the dark. This is why the journey of discovering hope leads me to Jesus.

This is what Jesus does.

Brings life.

Conquers death.

Sets the oppressed free.

Liberates the captives.

Gives sight to the blind.

You know, authentic hope.

The prayer team moved among the group leaders and there was a massive debrief and movement around following up with counseling and longer-term support groups. I couldn't do much more than that, as I was getting on a plane and flying back home that evening. But that night revealed the growing and desperate struggle of an entire generation with the darkness of despair. I still meet young people who are not so young anymore but who were there that night. We share something incredible. We share the same hope: *God's holiest intentions are to set us all free.* Free from self-harm, fear, shame, loathing, and death. To make us whole. That mass revealing was so hopeful to me because it reminded me that we don't have to live in the dark. And how many deep and despairing questions stay in the darkness of our own minds or under the floorboards of our own lives. We live in fear of asking them:

"Do I matter?"

"Am I enough?"

"What's the point?"

These are the questions we try to keep at bay the best we can. Busying ourselves with the day-to-day realities of paying bills and loving our families and occasionally numbing our existential angst with a few glasses of wine or fistfuls of carbs or whatever is most handy. But those questions still hide in the shadows, surfacing whenever we have a few moments to self-reflect or some time in relative silence to think a little deeper about our lives and our purpose and our world. *Thankfully*—we tell ourselves—*the pace of our modern lives leaves little to no time for this deeper thought.* Our calendars are jam-packed with activities—every hour stuffed full—and we try our best to squeeze some space in for exercise or a date night and call it a good week if we get a full eight hours of sleep at night. But then. Something happened. Something global.

Something that thrust us into a different pace, new ways of living, and opened the door to the shadow questions lurking in the dark like a robber hiding in the basement, finally sensing the time is ripe and running upstairs—using fear and cynicism and despair as his weapon to rob us of our peace.

COVID-19 and the ongoing consequences thrust the whole world into long seasons of space. Things were canceled, plans were put on hold, families were stuck together with little escape. All the normal patterns of our busy lives were interrupted and we finally had some time and space to . . . well, what did we think we would do? Some of us managed the first lockdown with some semblance of excitement. Finally, we'd have the time to read that book or do that DIY project or cook some decent meals. But after a month, all of those ideals were also dashed as maintaining even an ounce of hopeful, happy living during a global pandemic was lost.

The reality is that COVID drove the entire world into the kind of space that could have been used to really know ourselves and discover the hope that is intrinsic in our regular humanness and the possibilities of humans joining together in empathy and understanding and creative solutions to connect and be better people together. To be sure, there are stories where this did happen. But for the most part, we took that space and filled it with anything but reflection and honesty and genuine empathy or service. We squirmed our way out of that reflective space because in that space we were confronted with the ugly truth that within us, within our collective psyche, within our deepest fears and longings, was a cynical voice and a despairing conclusion. *What brings my life meaning? Why am I here? Do I matter? Does anyone really love me? What if people (even the people closest to me) really knew me—would they stay with me?* And we were terrified.

We watched way too many conspiracy shows (mostly called the news) that fed this fear. But now it's time to fight back. Really. We must fight back. Because if we leave cynicism unchecked and unconfronted and undefeated in our lives, businesses, churches, and systems, we will not make it. Despair will suck us into itself like a black hole absorbing all the matter around its circumference. Don't be fooled. Despair has a suction to it, a power. *And we will never defeat what we will not confront.* So let's get at it. Let's at least give ourselves a fighting chance in a culture that has almost completely given itself over to despair. Let's flip the script.

Cynicism is defined as "an inclination to believe that people are motivated purely by self-interest."[1] And despair is defined as "the complete loss or absence of hope."[2] In other words, cynicism is our lack of faith in people and despair is our lack of faith in everything else.

These things are deeply connected.

The loss of hope in the big possibilities of change is connected to the ways individual people have completely decimated our trust.

four

EVERYTHING IS CONNECTED

You know those elaborate displays of dominoes that people set up in crazy and wonderful patterns, and after all the work of setting them up they tap the first one and it taps the next one and then the whole thing cascades in this thrilling display of interconnectedness? There's a thrill as spectators watch the pattern emerge and the phenomenal courage of the creator taking the plunge of tapping that first one—and then everyone present experiences the sinking reality that all that work in setting this pattern up is undone in just a few seconds. Of course, there is also an excitement in explaining why it was set up in the first place.

Those feelings are at play all the time in the way our lives are interconnected. We spend a lot of energy and time setting things up separately. We do this constantly without much thought. We talk about getting in shape and we always mean physically. But we disconnect our physical selves from the mental and emotional parts necessary to be in total shape. We want to get it together spiritually but forget that our spirits are *in* our bodies and working within the realities of our parenting, relationships, daily decisions, and habits. We think our education is separate from our life experiences—except it isn't. What convinces us that we are complex and connected is that often one event can trigger and connect with all the other pieces, and within minutes or days or even a year, they cascade to launch us into a collapsing of all the parts.

I heard recently of a pastor—*another* famous pastor—who was caught having an extramarital affair. Unfortunately, this isn't new. I won't get into the details, but it included lying, cheating, hiding, secrets, hypocrisy, leadership abuse, and betrayal—all the things.

And here is the most tragic thing about it—no one was really surprised.

I mean, sure, people were a bit disappointed, but it really wasn't shocking. Because it seems that leaders, even godly ones, even famous ones, are all fake anyway. We assume that they lead out of selfish motives and for selfish gain. And the most horrific fact about this situation is not the behavior of one or two or even a dozen broken leaders but rather the vast majority of people who assume that's just how it is and there's nothing we can do about it. This is the harsh reality facing the underbelly of a number of people in public places who keep disappointing us. Politicians and pastors lead the pack; I think because there is a public expectation, a trust, that they will behave at least somewhat honestly and for the general good. To say this trust has been decimated is to understate it. This trust has so eroded that the very idea of "leader," which used to evoke positive, optimistic energy, now conjures up potential threats, hidden motives, and a kind of collectively held breath. We are afraid of leaders now. Afraid they will hurt us. Afraid they are the blueprint for the worst in all of us.

That, my friends, is cynicism breeding despair.

All normal emotions that are triggered by leaders betraying our trust (shock and outrage) have been sucked into the vacuum of despair because ultimately this is what we tell ourselves, even if under our breaths:

"It doesn't really matter anyway."

"We should have seen it coming."

And my personal favorite, "It's human nature."

We also keep our distance. Perhaps we don't realize that any public figure who betrays us is connected to every person in our lives who has betrayed us. That's part of the sting, the shock, the horror. Those personal disappointments and harm done to us bubble over and out of us onto "those people" whom we hate from a distance.

When we do look at the lives of the leaders who have disappointed us, it becomes glaringly obvious that they have lived fragmented ones. They have succumbed to a coping strategy that cynicism thrives in: *compartmentalization*. This is simply living separate lives in your various spheres of influence. Thinking that what you do and who you are at work is different from who you are at home. Or the way you engage in relationships with people in your daily life is completely different from the way you interact with people at church. Maybe you have beautiful values of generosity but are ruthless when it comes to investing. We segregate parts of ourselves.

COMPARTMENTALIZING OUR LIVES IS A SICKNESS

Exposing cynicism is no easy task. It reminds me of trying to combat bedbugs in a neighborhood infested with them. This is a true experience I had for several years while living in downtown Vancouver. Bedbugs were a problem. Not a small problem. A massive public problem. Whole hospitals and hotels had bed-burning affairs—a large-scale problem.

The thing about bedbugs that made them difficult to fight was their ability to remain invisible. It's almost impossible to find a bedbug without a major hunt. They only come out at night, and they feed on people's blood but don't actually hurt you when they bite, so you don't notice it while you are sleeping. But when you wake up, you have these bites all over your body (usually in groups of three). And it's disgusting. And you freak out. And you do all kinds of things—one of my friends insisted that if you put a jar around the bottom of your bed legs, the bedbugs couldn't get to you in bed. Turns out that doesn't work. Another friend insisted that putting certain essential oils on the mattress and pillows would keep them away—this also didn't work, although it did smell fantastic.

Mattresses would be burned and discarded, and new ones would come, and, alas, the bites continued. It was a nightmare. I believed bedbugs to be a demonic infestation—seriously. Straight from the pit of hell. I mean, what purpose do bedbugs even have in the complex, interconnected web of creation? They are like tiny little vampires coming to suck our blood and gross us out. They are also infectious, meaning they spread.

We had people visit us in Vancouver who took back more souvenirs than they had intended. Those little demonic bugs hid on their clothes and in the lining of their suitcases. And they soon infested new neighborhoods and bedrooms in other cities. Even writing this has exposed a deep trauma in my own life from this experience. During this season I was diligent. Bedbugs disgusted me, so I was on the lookout. I was always hosting people since that was my modus operandi for my church plant that met in my living room, but as soon as people exited, I got my tools assembled (vacuum cleaner, bleach/disinfectant spray) and got to work.

Once, I saw a bedbug. It's very unusual to spot one. But there it was. *On my bed*. On. My. Bed. I kid you not. So I did the only thing I could do. I stripped the bed, took the mattress and all the sheets, and immediately dragged it outside and called some friends to come help me burn it. I took all my clothes and sheets and put them in plastic bags and took them to the Laundromat, directly to a dryer. That's the surefire way to get rid of bedbugs (or if you have a really big freezer you can also use that). I disinfected my empty room—vacuuming every crevice and spraying something that *I* could hardly survive let alone a little bug. Then I ordered a new bed. A brand-new bed. That's what I did because I found one little bedbug on my bed.

You are probably shaking your head (hopefully chuckling) and wondering how I could have overreacted. But here is the thing. If you knew what I knew about bedbugs, you would know it wasn't an overreaction. The thing is, once you *spot* a bedbug, they have already taken over your bed. If you spot one, it means there are hundreds of them . . . somewhere. You might not find them. But you know they are there. Lurking in the darkness, just waiting for you to go to sleep.

So my repulsion and experience with bedbugs gave me more than a little trauma. It gave me an insight into how insidious darkness is. It also connected the dots between compartmentalizing our lives and thinking we've got it sorted. Complete thoroughness is required when it comes to bedbugs—and authenticity. Barriers must be broken down—even inside of us. Cynicism, it turns out, is a lot like bedbugs.

People aren't suddenly tempted with things like despair. Unless you are a famous academic or brooding artist, you won't be thinking much on an existential philosophical level—I mean, Kierkegaard was often right, but to contemplate his thoughts for too long makes your brain tired and then you aren't much fun at parties.

No, most of us are just trying to do our best. To stay positive. To work for change. To do the right thing. Most of our lives are not spent thinking about the deep philosophical reality of despair and the meaning of life; they are spent trying to do the dishes, laundry, school homework, keep the business afloat and our relationships alive, and experience some joy and friendship and give back a little. But after a few straight years of struggle and hardship, of worry and grief, and a cynical head start, we've landed way too close to the circumference of despair. And if we don't fight our way out of its suction, it will destroy us.

If you think the addiction crisis, loneliness epidemic, soaring depression, and anxiety rates are all just culminating by some cosmic coincidence at the same time and growing in steam through every conceivable industry, you are not facing it. The cynical despair I'm talking about is a full-blown existential angst. It has infested the retail store clerk, the stay-at-home dad, the up-and-coming lawyer. It has moved into all of our neighborhoods. We are collectively asking the questions that can lead us to the dark or can lead us through the dark and into the light. But how? Let's go a little further into where all this might have started.

five

ONE LITTLE PAMPHLET

Popular cynicism—the kind that undergirds our expectations of everyone we meet, especially leaders, to be self-serving jerks and unsurprisingly disappointing people—can be traced all the way back to the fifteenth century. Niccolò Machiavelli, a late-fifteenth-century statesman from Italy, wrote loads of different works (drama, history, etc.), but his last and most famous was *The Prince*. It was a brief political essay, framed as advice to monarchs about power (how to get it and how to keep it). No one really knows if he was being sincere or was writing a mockery intended to act more like a mirror to current leaders. It is true that "mirrors for princes" was a popular way of speaking to power since antiquity (Socrates was particularly famous for this technique). And many of the leaders Machiavelli was speaking to had disappointed him, thus explaining his having to write it while in exile. But the fact that no one could tell then, or even now, if it was a mockery or an instruction manual might give us a clue as to how much cynicism has already been working behind the scenes in human affairs.

Basically, the dominant themes are that it is better to be feared than to be loved, that there is no such thing as a "good" leader, only an effective one. Abandoning your own sense of morality for expedience and control is inevitable and enviable. The end always justifies the means (no matter how violent the means may be—albeit there is a small caveat that suggests if you do need to use violence, to do it fast and furious to get it out of the way). Nice guys never win. Powerful, terrible leaders have much to teach us, and though you don't need to be a great person, it helps if you appear to be better than you actually are.

The Catholics banned his book for more than two hundred years because of the one principle that kept coming up over and over again, namely, that being a good Christian was incompatible with being a good leader. Keep in mind that this all happened before the separation of church and state and that many of the most notoriously violent and terribly oppressive leaders were the head of the church at the time of their political careers.

I think Machiavelli was making a mockery out of his current leadership climate. In a letter to a friend after the pamphlet had been written, he said he "hoped people would learn the way to hell, in order to flee from it."

But it's safe to say that this one small, punchy political commentary did *a lot* to challenge and to change the popular conversations about power. Most historians say that what *The Prince* effectively did was change the dominant discussion from what should be to what is. And that was a good thing. Ultimately, society could stop playing around with dreams of saintly leaders and start dealing with the ones they had. It was a dose of reality. But it was laced with cynicism. And that cynical view of people would grow into a deadly disease.

The whole thing kind of reminds me of our current climate. The way we stack up people's actions in defense of their inhumane behaviors. The way we minimize the failings of leaders we admire or who have our best interests in mind and cancel those we decide need to be sacrificed on the altar of our righteousness. Who can tell which indiscretion will lead to failure and which one will lead to success? It's as though the set of principles to advise ruling monarchs in the fifteenth century has become a cultural playbook for society. Instead of leaders being taught this set of rules for achieving and maintaining power, everyone has learned it. Everyone has adopted the cynical realities of grasping and winning and leading with authority—good be damned. And if you object to this Machiavellian game of leadership? Or if you refuse to play the game of effective leadership? Then you're considered and treated as naive (which, let's be honest, is code for stupid). We've traded authenticity for manipulation.

I kind of wonder if reading Machiavelli's pamphlet during that time was like watching current politicians in ours. I'm not a political expert, or even really that interested in politics. But whenever I have tuned in to political speeches, I can't help but wonder if they've read *The Prince*. Or maybe to fifteenth-century culture it was more like watching the music video "This Is America" by Childish Gambino. With his lips he is speaking the narrative we all use to describe our freedoms and hopes and dreams, while the scenes in the video are filled with violence, emptiness, injustice, and pain. A mockery? We aren't sure either.

This kind of cynical attitude, whether a mockery or a genuine ideal, is the kind we've been swimming in for far too long. And it's time we confronted it—in our world for sure, but that, my friends, means starting with us.

six

HOW TO RESPOND

She was on a big dose of antidepressants. So high a dosage, in fact, that I started to lose her. She seemed vacant. Out for a coffee to catch up, I asked her about it. "Why are you taking such a high dose?"

"I can't stop crying," she explained. "The other day I was at the gym, on the treadmill, and I was weeping. The woman beside me was clearly worried and ended up leaving that treadmill to go to another one farther away! It was incredibly embarrassing."

I empathized but was still curious. "What are you crying about?"

"I'm not a 100 percent sure but I think it has to do with my husband's distance, my kids' dismissals, and my busy life with no real friendships. I feel lost. My life feels shallow and meaningless. What am I even doing with my life?"

As I thought through her list, it occurred to me that each item was worthy of tears. "Why don't you just let yourself cry?" I wondered out loud.

"Well, what will I say to the people around me when they are freaked out?" she asked.

"Why don't you just tell them you're human? That you are sad? That there is a lot for you to grieve right now?"

She said she'd stick to the medication.

Whatever the cause of our cultural despair (and it's multi-faceted for sure), it leaves us sad. And sad is not something we are really encouraged to feel. Happy is the only emotion worthy of emulation or experience, according to our culture. Confronting cynicism requires some willingness to grieve. For part of what makes cynicism so formidable an enemy is that it tends to use *some* truth but twists it to a terrible end.

"Pastors are all phonies."

"Professional athletes are all greedy."

"Politicians don't care about the people they serve."

"Christians are hypocrites."

"Men are jerks."

"Women are judgmental."

"Kids these days are selfish."

The reality is that many of those we had hoped would be better, would be different, would be the saintly leaders or people we long for, have only cemented the terrible hidden idea that everyone, including ourselves, is less than they appear. This revelation can be terribly sad.

I remember feeling this sadness, acutely, as I listened to the band Styx sing their hit song "Show Me the Way." I was much too young at the tender age of ten to grapple with the depth of truth these lyrics offered or its tragic inevitable sentiment, but it still haunted me. A biting pain in the cry, I heard it deeply. And it bears repeating.

How to Respond

Every night I say a prayer in the
hope that there's a heaven
And every day I'm more confused
as the saints turn into sinners

The lyrics are already sad. But they continue to echo the despair in our hearts.

All the heroes and legends I knew as
a child have fallen to idols of clay
And I feel this empty place inside so
afraid that I've lost my faith
Show me the way, show me the way[1]

I think what haunts me is the honesty. We've lost our way. Confused, we stumble around looking for someone to lead us somewhere we could get clean, get refreshed, be renewed. Find faith.

Cynicism is that kind of sad. The loss of hope we have in one another. Is there a better way to explain the way our world is falling apart? Every day our saints turn into sinners, and our leaders into self-serving jerks. Organizations and systems and governments and businesses and churches and nonprofits seem to routinely show they are only watching out for themselves—for their bottom line. It doesn't matter who they have to screw over. Corporations poison towns instead of owning their own mistakes; politicians lie their way to public office, concerned more with the optics than the truth; men abuse women; preachers preach about caring for the poor while wearing running shoes worth thousands of dollars; priests use their positions to sexually abuse those in their care; news outlets twist and sensationalize the truth to bump up their ratings. Is it any wonder we feel loss? We feel the suction of despair around every corner.

Scott Erickson (known on Instagram as Scott the Painter) speaks of a deep and sacred encounter he had at Disneyland. The surprise was in who it was with. "I entered into this section of the park where all the characters of *Inside Out* were standing. People were gathered around them and lined up to take their selfies with each character." In case you're unfamiliar, the characters from the Pixar movie *Inside Out* represent the four core human emotions: anger, joy, fear, and sadness. "There wasn't anything new about standing in line at Disney waiting to get a selfie with a movie character, but what took me by complete surprise was who the longest line was for. The line for people waiting to hug Sadness was winding around the corner. Out of all the core emotions, what people needed to embrace, what people wanted to embrace was Sadness." Scott goes on to explain his deep emotional impulse to get in line. "When it was finally my turn I hugged Sadness and felt something move deep inside me. I had *permission* to be sad. This moment liberated something inside me. I felt God there. The moment was sacred, holy."

What Scott encountered was this invitation to embrace his sadness, to acknowledge being sad as a genuine and important emotion in humanity. Our cultural obsession with stuffing sadness down has terrible consequences. Until we are ready to grieve our pain, hurt, disappointments, and despairing realities, we can never experience real hope. It will only be a vacant, shallow, and false hope that will not help us through the dark.[2]

Many years ago I felt led to gather a bunch of mission and church leaders working in the same geographic area to connect, pray, and dream together. It felt right. Why double our efforts and duplicate strategies? Why not unite and strategize to get smarter in our efforts to bring God's kingdom close and alleviate poverty? So I sent out the invites and was pleasantly surprised by the turnout in my living room. About a dozen ministries were represented. I shared what I thought was God's prompting to gather and unite us—and that's when it happened. The leaders turned on me.

"Who are you to call this meeting?" one of them asked.

"Don't you think we've already had this idea?" another one suggested.

Feeling threatened and diminished, I swallowed hard, gritted my teeth, told myself I'd be the bigger person, and continued on. But things went from bad to worse.

"I can't work with the people at this meeting—they are the problem!" One of them pointed a finger and recounted the split that resulted in their diminished ministry impact. It was a nightmare. Like bedbugs, the cynicism was spreading. It was awkward and unkind and visceral. It was cynicism and despair personified and voiced out loud. I had no idea what to do.

Ian, my coworker, was wide-eyed as it went on. We both were completely unprepared for how dark it was going to get. I was busy panicking and reverting into a shell of protection, saying things like, "Well, today is a brand-new day!" with a fake smile pasted on my face. But inside my head I whispered to myself, *It's okay, Danielle, you've got this* (ego) and *These people are crazy!* (blame) and *Is this even really happening?* (denial). The usual way we deal with angst. But Ian was too open and

41

soft-hearted for that kind of retreat. He started weeping. I mean legit, open ugly-crying. He was sobbing. He was expressing deep sorrow. And that sorrow showed itself that day in an absolute loud, blubbering mess on the living room floor. Sometimes sorrow has to come undone. Lament.

Everyone got quiet. Crickets quiet. But Ian didn't stop. He just kept weeping. And as he wept, we all felt something deep within us: sorrow. A deep, deep sorrow. And something began shifting in the room. People started to agree with the lament. What manifested itself as anger, blame, resentment, and accusation was really sadness.

A weighty sorrow came over us all. It came from somewhere deeper than just the grievances we had experienced from one another. There is a term the Bible uses to describe this kind of grief—it's called godly sorrow, and as the apostle Paul explained, "It leaves no regrets," and "It's the way to God" (2 Corinthians 7:10–11, author paraphrase). Jesus himself tried to explain the way of a "blessed" life in his core teachings in the Gospels (known as the Sermon on the Mount). He started with "poverty of spirit" and followed with "mourning." You are blessed when you are poor in spirit, when you can't help yourself! And when you mourn. You are blessed when you grieve.

What Jesus was telling us and what the good news has been consistent about since the beginning of all things is that in order to live a new way of life we have to die to old ones. Death to something involves a genuine acceptance and willingness to mourn. We can't just think our way into life-giving strategies; we have to feel our way as well. We have to allow the heart to grieve the present reality of cynical despair that has taken up residence in us. We have to recognize it and feel it. That's why covering it up and moving on without genuine remorse will not be enough. This explains why "stay hopeful" sticky notes don't quite do the trick. To reconcile us to the future possibilities of a new world we have to name and then grieve this present one. You want to experience hope that Indigenous peoples will rise from the ashes of systemic oppression and bring healing to the earth? Flip that hopeful belief over and grieve the realities of genocide and suffering found on the other side.

I'm so longing for hopeful reconciliation between the sexes, but it won't be found on glorious display until it is genuinely honest. The hope needed there will be found on the other side of pain, abuse, misogyny, and patriarchy. It'll be remorse that will hammer the boards together to display our hope to the world. African Americans have been holding on to hope for hundreds of years. And the way they've done it? They tell the truth. They grieve. They feel. And it's time to learn from what they've been demonstrating. The only way to a right relationship that battles racism is to confront the honest truth of our complicity and truly grieve it. Genuine hope can display its glory only on the framework of true repentance. When we've hammered the boards of honesty and humility together, they can form a solid backdrop from which we can paint a new piece of art with our lives.

So what do we do to rid ourselves of cynicism and despair? We confront it. We grieve together. We dig deep enough to uproot cynicism from the foundations of our minds and hearts.[3] And all that work doesn't start outside of us but inside of us all. If we are going to be free from cynicism's grip, we have got to dig deep. What cynicism threatens the most and uses as fuel for all its other work in our lives is central to who we are. *Our identity.*

seven

OUR CORE

Who are we? What is our purpose? Do we matter? These are the questions that cynicism tries to use against us. But they are also the core questions that, if answered, can liberate us. These questions are simmering underneath the surface of our lives because they are designed to. These questions are the very ones that can help us discover a truth that will lead us to hope. Not just for ourselves—although that is where it will begin. But it will also unlock a hopeful reality *between* us as well. Maybe George MacDonald said this best when he said, "Every question is a door handle."[1]

I think what we are most afraid of, which causes us to silence those deep questions, is that we will discover our own unworthiness, our own depravity. I think we believe that we are *not* good. In his book *Lies We Believe About God*, William Paul Young wrote, "Many of us believe that God sees us all as failures, wretches who are utterly depraved. We've written songs to reinforce our assumptions, penning lyrics about our own ugliness and separation. We think, When I hate myself, am I not simply agreeing with God?"[2] He goes on to describe a scene with his missionary, disciplinarian father. As his father was approaching him with obvious intent to hurt him, he started yelling out through blubbering cries, "Please don't . . . I'll be good! I'll be good! I'll be good!"

As he described the scene, I remember my own collage of experiences where the idea that I wasn't "good" was the identified problem. This lie about our badness, or lack of goodness, is so widespread and common that to challenge it creates a lot of pushback, even within our own selves. I remember having this revelation in my own deep recovery work. I always viewed addiction as a sin issue—grounded in being good or bad. I would pray, "Please, God, keep me good," and I developed a little code people would say, like "be good," when I would leave on a trip and the temptation would appear. One day I felt God tell me that I *was* good. That my goodness was not the problem. Sickness is not about being good or bad; it's about being unwell or unhealthy. Slowly, something began shifting in me.[3] Why are we so attached to the idea that we aren't good? I think it's an identity issue that exposes a core problem. This internal dread that plagues us with deep and often buried thoughts about our own unworthiness is the root that needs to be exposed. It's at this root that cynicism feeds and it's at that same root that cynicism can be rooted out and destroyed.

So let's start there. I had an epiphany about this very thing—my core identity. Many years before this struggle manifested, I had started using a little call-and-answer bedtime ritual with my youngest son. I would ask him, "Who made you?" And he would smile and answer, "God made me." And I would respond, "How did he make you?" And he would say, "He made me good." And I would agree. "He sure did, honey. He made you fearfully and wonderfully. He made you so very good!"

One night after this nightly exchange, as I exited his room, I found myself overcome with emotion. It wasn't that the moment was touching with my son, although it was. This particular unsettling was a dislodging of a belief. It occurred to me in that dark hallway, as I closed the door to my son's room, that I had believed, as the gospel truth, that I was *not* good. As we spoke the words together, it was like a light had shone on my own internal dialogue. I went back over many interviews that I had given over the years and heard myself explain my young teenage rebellion as evidence that I was a "bad kid" who had a special "gift for being bad." What became glaringly evident was that I believed at my core that I was *not* good. And I'm not alone. The church has been preaching the doctrine of total depravity for a long time. When I wiped away my tears, I discovered I had a lot of questions. Back in my own room I asked my husband, "When will our son turn bad?" I explained what had just happened and how beautiful it was and how it had moved me at a core level for some reason, and now I needed to know—when does that change? My husband responded in a deadpan voice, "I think it's around age seven or eight." And we both laughed. But I didn't keep laughing. I got curious.

When does it change? Or does it? And where does it say that exactly in the Bible? And who says so? And when did the doctrine of total depravity enter the Christian story and why? And so many other things started to unravel on the inside of me and make my brain hurt but ultimately led me to discover so many things I thought I knew that it turns out I didn't.

46

Including a lot about myself and my relationship with God.[4] As N. T. Wright put it,

> As with God so with the Bible; just because our tradition tells us that the Bible says and means one thing or another, that does not excuse us from the challenging task of studying it afresh in the light of the best knowledge we have about its world and context, to see whether these things are indeed so. For me the dynamic of a commitment to Scripture is not "we believe the Bible, so there is nothing more to be learned," but rather "we believe the Bible, so we had better discover all the things in it to which our traditions, including our 'protestant' or 'evangelical' traditions, which have supposed themselves to be 'biblical' but are sometimes demonstrably not, have made us blind."[5]

Without exaggeration, I believe that our deep problem with cynicism comes from our deepest problem: embracing ourselves. As Young said, "If I believe the deepest truth about me is worthlessness, then why are you surprised when I act like I'm worthless? Am I not at least being honest?"[6] It turns out that this revelation would be a strategic turning point in my faith. And the more I discover about this cynical lie, rooted in our core, the more I'm convinced it needs to be uprooted.

As I was floundering in this dislodging of a core belief, I found a book that would dare me to ask a question: What if I was not created in "original sin" but "original blessing"? Danielle Shroyer spends a whole book unpacking the origins of humanity and church history and the person of Jesus, and it blew my mind to rethink through the implications of what

I had been taught. I recommend you read it for yourself, but one of the most powerful connections to cynicism and despair in our dominant culture is this rooted belief in humanity's wretchedness. If the dominant way we view people (including ourselves) is through a lens of depravity, how might that affect the way we treat one another? I believe this is the crux of the seemingly endless cynical thinking that fuels our behaviors. If we can't view ourselves through a lens of worthiness, how can we view anyone else that way?

eight

HOW IT BEGAN AND HOW IT ENDS

Are you ready to have your mind blown? Buckle your seat belt, friend. You might even want to carve out a few extra hours in your schedule today to just sit with this. Journal. Doodle. Let it really sink in.

This business of the Western church making sin a bigger deal—making it *foundational*—making it more than the Bible makes it, influenced my self-understanding, and I expect it's shaped yours too. Danielle Shroyer explained, "So here's the most basic church history lesson I can muster for you: in 1054, the church split, and when they did, they chose different boxes. The East chose death, and the West chose sin. And ever since that fork in the road, Western Christianity has organized its theology around the assumption that sin is the pivotal reality."[1]

At our core, the Western church insisted, we were bad. Theologians began to read the Bible through the lens of depravity. Human badness was at the heart of every problem.

Jump forward a few centuries and Jonathan Edwards sparked the Great Awakening in America with a sermon entitled "Sinners in the Hands of an Angry God." In that message he described how God views us like we view a spider. We see a disgusting creature that we want to destroy. It's actually pretty powerful rhetoric but not the kind of power that leads us to loving relationships. It's the kind of power that leads us to religious fear. "He looks upon you as worthy of nothing else, but to be cast into the fire; he is of purer eyes than to bear to have you in his sight; you are ten thousand times so abominable in his eyes as the most hateful venomous serpent is in ours."[2] Catchy, right?

Ever since then, most of American/Western religion seems to be varying exercises in fear. Fear of being left behind when God finally destroys the earth by fire. Fear of not being good enough to earn God's favor. Fear that if we are different or broken or sinful we will be sent to an everlasting torment designed for the enemies of God. Fear of breaking the rules and losing the blessing. Read Western church history and you will discover what we could easily subtitle it: Centuries of Wrath, Punishment, and Exclusion. Brian Zahnd, in his book *Sinners in the Hands of a Loving God: The Scandalous Truth of the Very Good News*, put it this way: "Edwards preached that sermon, and it has left its mark on the religious imagination of America. It is generally regarded as the most important sermon in American history. And this is a tragedy. It's regrettable this sermon has shaped the American vision of God for nearly three centuries." Regrettable indeed. Because God does not see us this way.

There is only one way that our theological self-loathing could end—and it's in the person of *Jesus*.

It would take me years to discover that God sees me *the exact opposite* way that Jonathan Edwards suggested and my religious upbringing had led me to believe. No doubt this is what Jesus modeled so well. In the stories of his life it becomes obvious that he saw differently than everyone else. He saw through the religious, cultural, and personal baggage and right into people's core. He saw *who they really were.* And when he saw who they really were, he had deep love for them. The radical nature of this love demonstrated by Jesus in his life on earth cannot be overstated. Also, if you struggle (like many Western Christians do) with the idea that how Jesus sees us is different from how God (the Father) sees us, please know this: it's not true. Zahnd explained, "People have never seen God until they see Jesus. Every other portrait of God, from whatever source, is subordinate to the revelation of God given to us in Jesus Christ. Jesus is the Word of God, the Logos of God, the Logic of God in the form of human flesh. Christians are to believe in the perfect, infallible, inerrant Word of God—and his name is Jesus."[3]

And consider his example. He went to Romans (enemies), demon-possessed men (evil), Gentiles (judged), Jews (chosen), religious (included), nonreligious (excluded), female (subservient), foreigners (rejected), kings (authorities), poor (unwanted), and rich (arrogant). He demonstrated that the good news is that God is radical and inclusive love. That absolutely everyone is invited to the kingdom. And this might be the truly amazing part—the most beautiful part, the part that could bring me to tears as I type it out. *He loves me right now.* There is nothing I can do or not do, nowhere I could go or not go, that would separate me from the love of God. That's literally a Bible verse (you can read the whole chapter in Romans 8). And what does that mean? Well, this is the incredibly beautiful news about God: His love is not just sentimental emotion void of power. His love is a power that can transform us. His blazing love can reveal all the junk and distortion, the baggage and the religion, the mindset and the racism, the abuse and the disfigurement of our lives (we call that *sin*) and liberate us to see *who we really are* and were always meant to be from the start, and empower us to become who we already are in him. Jesus wants us to be our truest selves. I know this is a lot to take in. You may need to read it again.

Sometimes what we are afraid of is that this radical message of love and inclusion will lead us to think that *we* are the solution to our troubles. I think genuine followers of Jesus are worried about being "soft on sin" not because they are judgmental but because they want to be honest. There is no doubt that sin is the problem. Greed, lust, injustice, racism, misogyny, and abuse are just a few outworkings of sin in the world. But here is the distinction that can liberate us from a diseased core: we are not sin. We are God's children. Sin is our enemy. Our collective enemy. The distinction is important. If we confuse our identity with our enemy, we despair. Now, part of the problem is our varying definitions of sin. Sin (from Scripture) literally means to "miss the mark." When we talk about sin, we mean anything from willful disobedience against God to every injustice and brokenness in the world. Sin is something that happens *in* us but also something that happens *to* us. Sin is what separates us from God. To be more specific, sin is what tells us we are separate from God. But sin is a liar. It turns out God has never kept his distance. The ancient Hebrew songwriter put it best:

"Where can I go from your Spirit? . . . If I go up to the heavens, you are there; if I make my bed in the depths . . . even there your hand will guide me" (Psalms 139:7–8,10). Or in case we think it's just poetic license, the apostle Paul put it like this: "For I am convinced that neither death nor life, neither angels nor demons, neither the present nor the future, nor any powers, neither height nor depth, nor anything else in all creation, will be able to separate us from the love of God that is in Christ Jesus our Lord" (Romans 8:38–39). Sin's deceptive power fuels another deep-seated lie that feeds cynicism: we are alone. This old and toxic idea that we are our sin pits God against us. But it turns out we share a common enemy. God is liberating us to fight against sin with him. Goodbye to shame, fear, guilt, condemnation, self-harming behaviors, and toxic egos. Hello to fresh hope. "When we say, 'Jesus died for our sins' within a message about how to escape this nasty old world and go to heaven, it means one thing. When we say, 'Jesus died for our sins' within a message about God the creator rescuing his creation from corruption, decay, and death, and rescuing us to be part of that, it means something significantly different."[4] Young unpacked the implications this way:

> God doesn't have a low view of humanity, because God knows the truth about us. God is not fooled by all the lies we have told ourselves and each other. Jesus is the truth about who we are—fully human, fully alive. Deeper than all the hurt and broken bits and pieces is a "very good" creation, and we were created in the image and likeness of God. But we have become blind in the deceit-darkness we believe. It is time for us to stop agreeing with these devastating lies.[5]

I remember the airplane seat I was sitting in when the deep truth sank into my heart—12F. I was midflight, exploring and contemplating these mind-blowing ideas of goodness and sacredness and sin. A song began to play that simply took my breath away. I was trying to read but soon my eyes had filled with tears and reading was out of the question. I lowered my book and shut my eyes, letting the tears flow. Jon sang, I listened to the refrain, "All of God's children, shining underneath."[6] This deep thought that underneath all of my own pain, shame, grief, and guilt, underneath the darkest brokenness in me, was something sacred—well, this thought flooded my heart and overwhelmed my mind. Soon I began to think of all the people I had journeyed with. People who struggled under the weight of their sin. People who I knew were carrying an exhausting burden of unworthiness. Their faces started to form a collage in my mind. Moms who had lost their children to social services because of their addiction and pain. Men who kept hurting people they loved with their anger. So many friends despairing with addiction. The women who can't get out of bed, depression literally holding them down. Jon continued singing, "Underneath these wars. Underneath these walls. Underneath the bullet holes. I still don't know who we are. But it's shining underneath."

And I wept. I wept for all of us. I wept that we have allowed sin to have the first and final word. I cried that I had lost so much time and so much joy by believing sin. This grief came as a strange mixture of relief and joy. As the revelation came, I began to see more clearly that this misunderstanding of sin was fueling so much of our self-destructive behaviors. It simultaneously occurred to me that seeing God's love as the first and final word, the one that overcomes sin and conquers it, was the power I needed to hope for humanity again. As the song goes, "I believe in a world that's beyond me. I believe in a world I ain't seen. Past the glass, and shotgun shacks, and violent, faceless, racist facts. I believe in a world that's made clean."

There is a deep level of good news happening here if you are paying attention. There's a word *underneath* the word. A deeper level opening for us to enter. Or as Aslan put it in the Chronicles of Narnia when the young daughters of Eve were so confused about the slain lion being alive, "There is a magic deeper still."[7] And what is it? What is this deeper magic? It's the truth that love is a power greater than any other. And that you are loved. You are made from love. Made for love. Made in love. And by love. I mean that you are wanted, received, worthy, whole, sacred, and complete. I guess in a way I'm just reliving my son's nighttime ritual with you. Who made you? God made you. And how did he make you? He made you good. This is the great invitation of Jesus. To discover the deeper magic, the light shining underneath. To find an answer to the questions we are all avoiding and despairing about. Who are you? You are beloved. These are the very places that will lead us to a sacred core identity. And it's this confrontation that can be the most liberating of all.

nine

WHO WE ARE AND WHO WE AREN'T

Cynicism is rooted in the very foundation of our lives—at our core. So let's go deeper. We were made for goodness and out of goodness. The creation accounts in Genesis 1 and 2 are both filled with love.[1] Genesis 1:2 says, "The Spirit of God was hovering over the waters." The word "hover" is the same word used to describe a mother hen lovingly watching over her young, warming the eggs and protecting the hatchlings. Just in the creation account, the phrase "God saw that it was good" is written five times, and "it was very good" after the sixth day (after he created humanity) (Genesis 1:10, 12, 18, 21, 25, 31). I urge you to read Psalm 139. All of it. It reminds us that we are fearfully and wonderfully made. Our life stories and our human story does not begin in sin but in blessing.

You may be thinking, *Well, if that's the case, what do I need saving from?* I'm convinced that most Christian theology from the last few hundred years begins to tell the gospel story at

Genesis 3 instead of Genesis 1 because they think it makes the news of salvation better. In their book *Reframation*, Alan Hirsch and Mark Nelson explained,

> If we reduce the gospel by beginning with the problem, then the whole search for God becomes a negative problem-solving journey. And to those who are desperately searching for something more, reducing the good news to problem-solving and moralism presents itself as an exercise in futility.[2]

This misconception, or what Alan and Mark would call a "reduced idea" of God's plan and purpose, might also help us understand why Christians keep using Hallmark anecdotes as gospel truth.

Things *don't* always happen for a divine reason or children wouldn't starve to death.

God is *not* in control of everything or we wouldn't be free to choose—and that'd be some kind of weird, cosmic *Truman Show*, not a story of reconciliation.

And joy *isn't* always a choice.

Just saying.

A simplistic, reduced view of the epic story of divine love finds it easier to pit God against humanity and humanity against God. But that is not the gospel. It turns out that God has never been an enemy of humanity—despite our crazy ideas and religious inconsistencies and even our rebellion and pride. God has consistently been leading us to understand and experience that he is good and he is with us. No matter what.

Jesus is the pinnacle of this revelation and he went all the way to the cross in the ultimate act of compassion to convince us once and for all that he is not angry—he is love. I memorized Colossians 1:21–22 when I first encountered Jesus because I thought it summed up my testimony nicely: "Once you were alienated from God and were enemies in your minds because of your evil behavior. But now he has reconciled you by Christ's physical body through death to present you holy in his sight, without blemish and free from accusation." For more than twenty years I quoted that verse and never really understood it, until recently.

Over the last few years, there was one phrase that started to stand out: "In your minds." I was an enemy of God—*in my own mind*. God has never been an enemy of mine. God has no human enemies. When I first shared this idea on social media, there was a lot of pushback. Some people were so furious that I was suggesting God wasn't angry that it was a little, well, disturbing. This idea is so deeply lodged within our understanding of the gospel that it's no wonder fear, guilt, and shame are the primary ways we communicate about God. Romans 5:10 is often cited as evidence that we are in fact God's enemies because it asserts that our friendship with God was restored by the death of his Son while we were still his enemies. But as I went back and read through the whole chapter, I was again reminded that we are being rescued from what we thought was true about God—that he is full of judgment and that we are simply destined to suffer his wrath. The whole chapter (and book, for that matter) is trying to tell us that Jesus came to show us the real face of God. And it's love. And that love is active and moving and working on our behalf even when we pit ourselves against God or believe we are separate from him. Roman 5:8 says, "While we were still sinners, Christ died for us," and helps sum this up pretty nicely. If God was angry or our enemy, he would have waited to demonstrate his extravagant love for us. But he didn't. Because it's not true. And this is so clear to me now and so exciting and revolutionary that I want to scream it from every mountaintop in the world: God has no human enemies! He is not against you; he is not mad at you. He is not even perpetually disappointed (which is the worst of the views, in my opinion). God is love. God is for you. God made you. God knows you. God loves you. God can liberate you from sin. Why did Jesus come? Jesus did not come to change the mind of God about humanity. It didn't need changing. God has organically, inherently loved what God created from the moment God created it. Jesus came to change the mind of humanity about God.[3]

Recently I was listening to my friend (and theologian) Bob Ekblad explain how he helps people who have been beaten down by the world understand what God wants to do in their lives. And in this particular case he was in a conversation with a man who was in prison. He used a very famous passage of Scripture from the same book we've been talking about. Romans is a theological letter that the apostle Paul wrote to explain the essentials of Jesus-centered faith over religious tradition. In Romans 7:15–20, Paul outlined the human dilemma.

> I do not understand what I do. For what I want to do I do not do, but what I hate I do. And if I do what I do not want to do, I agree that the law is good. As it is, it is no longer I myself who do it, but it is sin living in me. For I know that good itself does not dwell in me, that is, in my sinful nature. For I have the desire to do what is good, but I cannot carry

it out. For I do not do the good I want to do, but the evil I do not want to do—this I keep on doing. Now if I do what I do not want to do, it is no longer I who do it, but it is sin living in me that does it.

Read that last line again. "Now if I do what I do not want to do, it is no longer I who do it, but it is *sin living in me* that does it." Depravity occurs when our human operating system (our flesh / sinful nature) has been taken over by a foreign power—a virus that has corrupted our core. Cancer might be a useful metaphor. Cancer distorts our own cells to fight against us. It embeds itself into our operating system in order to kill us. That's a good descriptor of what sin does. Distorts and embeds, convincing us that we are the disease. The result is a killing, stealing, and destroying of ourselves and our place in this world (John 10:10). This analogy also connotes the kind of emotional energy required to fight back.

Back to the prison: after they read that passage of Scripture, Bob asked the man, "So, can you relate?"

Looking Bob in the eye, the man confirmed, "It pretty much describes my whole life situation. It's why I'm *here*."

Then Bob wondered aloud, "If there was a cure for this 'sin nature' or 'foreign enemy' that keeps forcing us to do what we don't want to do, would you want it?"

The man studied Bob, waiting to see where he was going.

Bob continued, "If God could help liberate you from this predicament, would you want that?"

Who wouldn't?!

"Yes," the man replied. "Of course I would."

This possibility of being liberated from "our body of death" is the best news anyone has ever heard. *It really is.* This is what makes the gospel such good news in a culture that simply cannot believe it is possible to change. Who can't relate to feeling trapped in an inner war with ourselves? Paul said "O wretched man that I am!" not as a value statement of identity but as an emotional description of his pain (Romans 7:24 NKJV). We feel like we are at war with ourselves but we are really at war with sin. The distinction may sound small but I think it's essential.

Our salvation is a restoration operation. We are saved by the powerful love of Jesus that will liberate us at our core from the virus of sin. The Spirit of Jesus is our treatment plan for the cancer of sin.

When cynicism attaches itself to our core like a virus, it begins to spread throughout our entire operating system. We start to believe the despairing lies that *we* suck. That *we* are terrible. That *we* are bad. That everyone is bad. If we are already religious and struggling with sin, equating our identity with sin convinces us that *we* are hypocrites who deserve punishment. Sometimes we simply deny these thoughts and feelings. But we still wonder. Other times we work ourselves to death trying to prove these inner voices wrong. We keep busy. We get disciplined. We turn super religious.

This explains why self-help isn't the kind that we need. Self-help is a software answer to a hardware problem. We need a restoration of existing materials. Files that were loaded at the start of our lives. We need an engineer who knows how to recover what already exists—not just load on more things to try to cover our problems with a fancy new system. This is where Paul released the ultimately revolutionary news: "Thanks be to God, who delivers me through Jesus Christ our Lord!"

(Romans 7:25). Who made you? God did. And how did he make you? He made you good. And that is the gospel truth.

The distinction of sin being a virus/enemy and our own selves being image bearers may sound a little like playing with semantics. But it isn't. It's a deep shift. At a core level, if our hatred of our sin is related to who we are, *sin wins*. We end up hating ourselves. And we end up believing that God hates us as well. How much of what has looked like "Christian devotion" has just been self-loathing? This is sin winning no matter how much religious talk we wrap it in. To believe that other people are evil, or even enemies of God, to obsess about burning in hell, and to condemn others to that kind of fate in the name of God is what I call a theology of despair.

Besides the good news being a restoration operation (restoring us to our original identity and purpose) and a mysterious, big news story about the unfathomable creative love (restoring our awe of God), it's also a discovery that salvation offers us a way to become our truest selves. And this is what can change the game on the lie that cynicism tries to spread.

ten

SORROW, NOT DEFEAT

Embracing our humanity is difficult. Really. The fact that Jesus became human to demonstrate that even in the limiting reality of our humanness we still have choices and the capacity to help shape the world into something more beautiful is itself mind-blowing.

Despair will tell you that you can't fix things you can't control. Being human has limitations, frustrations, and a million things you can't do. The world is not okay, despite my telling myself that all will be well and whispering that sentiment to the universe. The fact is, based on just my everyday experiences, I can see that the world is not doing well. And it's in this soft, vulnerable place where despair lurks. And very quickly, despair will trick you to believe that what you feel is not sorrow but defeat.

This is where despair is a liar. A big, fat, pants-on-fire liar to be sure. Because mourning and genuine sorrow at the condition of the world (even our inner worlds) is not despair—it's honesty. This is where false hope really plays a number on us. We've been trying to "be hopeful" by convincing ourselves that things aren't as bad as they look. But this kind of hope has been harmful because things are often as bad as they look—if not worse. Hope, when it isn't honest, is not helpful.

Discerning between sorrow and despair is deeply spiritual work. It's not something we can do ourselves. Left to our own devices our hearts can be deceived. We need power, strength, and community to help us navigate this deep space. And this is where we can get some help from Jesus.

Jesus spent time with God. It sounds so simple and obvious. It feels almost childlike to say this but let me say it again, *Jesus spent time with God*. By himself. Hours. What was he doing exactly? When he taught on prayer in Matthew 6, he instructed us not to do it publicly but privately. Why? He talked about the "secret place" where we commune with God the Father, and that we can be "delivered from evil" and "guided through temptation," and all kinds of other ways of fighting against despair, including divine daily provision.

I've been working on my inherent bias when approaching Scripture. What I mean is that most of the people I have learned from are from my culture, background, race, and socioeconomic group. It's like I'm in a theological echo chamber. To combat this pull toward sameness, I signed up for a course with Freedom Road. Lisa Sharon Harper and René August led "Decolonizing the Bible." One of the texts we took a deep look into was the Lord's Prayer. It turns out what I thought was mostly devotional was much more like spiritual resistance training. Lisa explained the Roman strategy to ensure dependency on colonized people by using salt to deaden the local fields. They'd distribute food to the people as "providers" of their needs. Roman soldiers would pull a cart through the towns giving "daily bread" to keep the people dependent on them. In the Lord's Prayer, Jesus suggested that we pray for our daily bread to come not from Rome but from God. In using the same term as the rations provided by an occupying force, Jesus was asking his disciples to think differently about the kind of kingdom God was offering. What kind of emotions might this have produced in the disciples? What kind of interpretation might this evoke in the people listening to Jesus' prayer instructions? What does it do inside of you?

Jesus was asking his followers, then and now, to allow God to be their provision. To imagine and pray for a world that is dependent not on an empire, an economy, a political ideology, but on the Son of Man. It's not a shallow dismissal of oppression; it's a confrontation of it. When you pray every day, go to the secret place *where God hears you.* This is a direct refute of religious sects at the time who taught that God would only hear pious prayers offered along with proper sacrifices in the synagogues through the priestly line. The God who Jesus was invoking is the Father of us all—accessible by the least of us, in our own homes. If it's access to a power greater than ourselves that we need, we have it. No need to look any further, offer any elaborate sacrifices, or make pious declarations in specific places. Just ask. Ask the Father for the kingdom. And it's yours. For many of us who have been raised in a culture that champions individualism and autonomy, this might be difficult to fully understand. Part of our cynicism is the lie that nothing can change. That God doesn't hear us and even if he does it can't change anything. This is what makes the invitation of Jesus so hopeful.

Jesus offered an honesty to hope that infuses it with the

possibility of a different future. Far from removing the difficulties or even just reframing them, Jesus confronted them and embraced them as inevitable parts of being human. It is a gritty hope that doesn't ignore the hard bits but takes them head-on. It is a hope that is up to the task of believing that this world God has made will be set right. As Martin Luther King Jr. put it, "We shall overcome because the arc of the moral universe is long but it bends toward justice."[1]

Jesus assures people who feel forgotten and rejected and unworthy that they have direct access to God. There is a power greater than them available to help them. Every single addict who comes to the end of themselves, who loathes their very existence, and who is led to their knees to pray a prayer of surrender knows the relief of accessing a power that they simply do not have themselves. This access is what I mean about an authentic hope. It's not hope that we can do better on our own. The hope we really need is not sourced from inside of us. It is given to us through a source much more powerful than us. God doesn't want us to deny our humanity to get access to this divine hope—quite the opposite. The access comes when we accept our humanity, our limitations, emotions, frustrations, and come with them to receive what we need for today.

Jesus' most-used description of himself in the gospel accounts is this title: the Son of Man. This title is literally translated "the human one." Jesus was not ashamed of his humanity. He put it on and referred to himself, every chance he had, as the human one. Apparently, the shame and self-loathing of our humanity is not natural or necessary.

His behavior continued to suggest an embracing of humanness, not a rejection of it.

He publicly wept over the condition of the people he came to save. He went out of his way to get in the way of injustice and pain, exclusion and evil. Even after his death and resurrection, Jesus confronted the disciples with the truth of their limitations and fear. He wasn't simply brushing off their humanity—he was healing them, embracing them, and offering them a way of being more human in this world by allowing the kingdom to invade more and more of them.

Isn't this what he did with Peter in the final scene of the Gospels? After Peter's very public denial at the crucifixion, the story picks up with his return to fishing. Jesus approached the shore and repeated the first miracle Peter had experienced. It was about catching fish. This time Peter realized that it was Jesus, and he jumped overboard and ran directly to Jesus, where he expressed his uncleanness—and even as we read the account, we can agree that Peter was unworthy. He couldn't even do what he promised Jesus directly—he could not stay faithful for one night. Jesus then asked him a question. "Peter, do you love me?" Peter answered, "Of course, Lord, you know I love you." "Then feed my sheep" (John 21:17, author paraphrase). Jesus asked the question three times while building a fire. In case it escaped your notice, look at this passage again and consider that it was over a fire that Peter denied Jesus exactly three times. And here they were, at a fire again, and the question was asked three times. The point?

The point is about hope and forgiveness and restoration. And Peter. Peter couldn't be hopeful about the future if he wasn't honest about the past. Neither can we. Theologian Dietrich Bonhoeffer called this idea of Christianity—this hopeful gloss-over of the depth of our own misery and capacity for culpability and sin—"Cheap grace."[2] And he doesn't mean we should be more religious and pious and sacrificial—he means we need to be more *honest*. Jesus didn't just move on as though Peter's denial didn't happen. He didn't need Peter to grovel; he wanted Peter to heal.

We are often so afraid of our brokenness that we try to hide it. And that's where cynicism (our loss of hope in ourselves) begins to fester and grow. And that's what bears the fruit of despair in our thoughts, actions, and relationships. But how did we get so ashamed of ourselves? And how can we get more honest?

Scripture says that godly sorrow is what leads us to repentance. The word *repentance* comes from the Greek word *metanoia*, which means "to change the way we see." It's to have our minds blown. In their book *Reframation*, Hirsch and Nelson explain their search that led them to write about what is essentially a call for the church to shift their view of God and humanity (repentance). They explained,

> As lovers of all things God, we have kept our hearts in a state of holy restlessness in a search for a God big enough to change everything. We refuse to settle for the initial, partial experience of God we had when we first came to believe. We seek to know God as he wished to be known . . . through ever-expanding and enchanting frames, through eyes of wonder and love, believing with Augustine that "If you understand, it is not God." God is ever greater, always bigger, than anything we think we know of him.[3]

Godly sorrow is not just wallowing in our sin, being sorry for what we've done wrong; it's a ticket into the depth of God's heart—it's a way of entering into Jesus' life. Denial, even hopeful denial, will not cure us from despair—it will deepen its impact. But honesty—honesty is a core place.

And honesty is where we begin to make a new world together. And this is the ultimate irony. The same place we can begin is the same place we can end. We have to decide. And this ability to choose is ultimately the way we defeat despair and usher in hope as a way of life.

That's why in the most famous speech of all time—when Jesus gave his recipe for what really makes a blessed life and the first two "blessings" include being poor in spirit and mourning —we struggle to make sense of his words. I think we are all tempted to believe Jesus was some kind of alien just visiting this planet, and not the human being he really was. How is it possible that the blessed life is through these things? This is literally the opposite of what we've seen and heard our entire lives. How could this be? To even suggest that to live a truly blessed life is to mourn—well, we just don't get it. We scoff at the ludicrous idea of it. How does mourning lead to comfort? This is the difficulty.[4]

Allow me to introduce you to a priest with AIDS. Christo works with World Vision International as a specialist who has trained thousands of faith-based communities in how to welcome and embrace people suffering with infectious diseases. I interviewed him in an episode of a podcast I did called *Right Side Up*.[5] He explained that when he was diagnosed, he was shocked and afraid and desperate. What was he going to do? How can you be a priest with AIDS? It happened during the AIDS crisis in South Africa, and he was really confused about why God had called him as a priest and then allowed him to get a disease that was sure to kill him and would make him despised until then. He describes sitting in St. George's Cathedral in Cape Town, South Africa, trying to pray. He looked up and saw right at the front of the church a massive painting of Christ. But it was like nothing he had ever seen before. The painting was by the artist Maxwell Lawton and entitled *Man of Sorrows: Christ with AIDS.* It revealed Christ suffering with AIDS. And written over top of the image in the Zulu language was the Beatitudes. "Blessed are the poor in spirit . . ."

In this moment he felt God speak to him. Christo says he felt an invitation to participate with God in suffering and find comfort and hope there. Although it's a mystery, it's a glimpse into the way of Jesus to bring meaning and possibility even out of tragic and despairing situations.[6]

Hope is not the absence of suffering; it's the presence of God in the midst of it.

Allowing our hearts to open to the mysterious way of God drawing near, and to feel the sorrow of our own loss, opens us to the life of Jesus. How many of us think that sorrow is despair? How many of us force our emotions to settle, and stop our deep questions, and steer ourselves away from the passionate cry on the inside of us? Our shrinking back from our honest selves, real questions, and genuine sorrow is often what limits us from encountering the divine. For Christo, it was that moment when something shifted inside of him, and he began working on ways to serve those most excluded and persecuted—orphans with AIDS—to be welcomed and embraced, healed and included. When I spoke with Christo, the thing that stood out to me the most was how he exudes hope. He is hopeful even though he has known and seen a lot of despair. The difference is that his hope isn't denial—it's the presence of God in the midst of the suffering. Christo has found Jesus and found how to access Jesus at the center of his darkness.

This is how you can be a realist and be hopeful. Entering into honesty with God by confronting our pain and fear is how we stop the cynical thoughts and prevent ourselves from slipping into despair. I printed a copy of *Christ with AIDS* and put it up in my office. When I'm tempted to give up, go shallow, stuff down my feelings, pretend to be okay when I'm not, or hide my life from others (including God), I glance up at that painting and think back to my conversations with Christo. It usually takes only a few minutes for me to touch what I need most. Hope.

eleven

ENDING THE WAR WITHIN

Jenna counsels people. All kinds of people. Leaders, mothers, fathers, pastors, other counselors. But she's been frustrated for much of her professional life at a disconnect at people's core. Let's use the example of the sex addict. Of all the people she helps, she believes the sex addict has it the hardest. Because sex addiction is so difficult to bring into the open for obvious reasons, it's often the hardest to deal with. She has tried all kinds of counseling techniques but has realized that most of them were connected to behavioral change (stop doing that), or led to even more self-loathing (I'm just a broken and bad person). She was despairing because she really didn't see much transformation happening—and it wasn't for a lack of trying. It wasn't for a lack of faith. But then she discovered something that actually worked. And by "worked," I mean that it produced transformational change in her clients whenever she used this system.

This strategic system is called IFS (Internal Family Systems). Jenna Riemersma is the founder and clinical director of the Atlanta Center for Relational Healing.[1] I encourage you to visit their website to hear her explain IFS in a captivating video, but for now the basic idea is this:

- You have a true self at your core that is good.
- When you experience pain (trauma), parts of you are put in "exile" because we don't like pain.
- Other parts of you rise up to deal with these exiles.

In Internal Family Systems theory these are called "managers" or "firefighters." Managers are the ones who are trying hard to control your behavior, and firefighters are trying to extinguish the pain. Ultimately, all the parts are essentially good but are stuck in roles (burdened) that keep you from being free to live out of your core self.

Jenna explained to me that when she was trained by IFS founder Dr. Richard Schwartz, she knew instinctively that this resonated with the gospel message from the Scriptures. As a counselor, she had more experience than she wanted with Christians who were living fragmented and shame-filled lives. They were stuck in harmful, sinful behaviors, and self-loathing was not helping them get free—it was actually causing them further harm. She recognized the compassionate impulse of Jesus, who helped people admit the truth and embrace love (radical acceptance) as the way to be reconciled and healed.[2]

I agree. I see that in Jesus. Not an unwillingness to deny the truth but rather an acceptance that makes the truth transformative. What Jenna has discovered is central to the foundational shift required to free us from many things, cynicism included.

People are despairing when it comes to mastering themselves. And here is why. We are fragmented. Much like Romans 7 suggests we are constantly at war with ourselves, cynicism tells us regularly and methodically that this is simply what it means to be human.

Years ago I did some deep recovery work with a sponsor. "Danielle," she said as we sipped coffee, "the self you show the world doesn't really match up with who you are. In public you give off this fearless attitude. But in the work you've done it seems like what's really driving you, at your core, is fear."

I responded with an eye roll and answered, "Welcome to the human dilemma."

I thought that I was expressing a deep truth that everyone was too afraid to admit.

She looked at me and responded, "Do you really believe that bullshit?"

I was a bit flustered. I really did believe it. I assumed that the hypocrisy I had adopted as a survival mechanism was what everyone else did too. I thought it was revolutionary for me to humbly accept it and do the best I could anyway. But she called it for what it was. Cynicism had crept into my *core* and told me I could never really be as good or as free or as whole as my image. That conversation made me see for the first time that what I was using as an excuse for my own fragmentation was not intellectual and philosophical freedom. Rather, it was a lie—the direct result of a cynical virus. Total bullshit indeed.

Now, in my case, at that time, the issues weren't out of

control. I wasn't stealing money or cheating on my spouse or anything that I could be busted for and fall from a public platform over. No, those are glaringly obvious "out of control" behaviors indicative of a massive system shutdown—much harder to deny (although, obviously, people do). Rather, what my friend pointed out were the subtle disconnects. The small acceptance of living in a way that I didn't agree with (denial). The ideals that I trumpeted since my early calling that I had quietly put away, convinced they would never happen (shame). My reluctance to take on systems that were unjust because of the seeming inevitability of their success (fear). My refusal to get help for my own trauma while I helped others through theirs (codependency). For the most part I had chalked much of these things up to maturity and experience. For sure, when you are fighting against systems and structures—whether injustice or ignorance—there is simply a fatigue that can set in. I've been fighting against human trafficking and sexual exploitation for decades. I've been fighting against religious systems and toxic cultures that abuse and limit people—unhelpful processes that hold people back from their calling and potential. I've been fighting against poverty and exclusion, and I've been fighting my own internal voices of shame. I told myself it was this. It was compassion burnout. I was tired of fighting. It was the inevitable consequence of watching people struggle and fail as I had so many times.

But as I got more honest, I realized that I had been allowing cynicism to take root in my core identity, using "inevitable failure" to let myself off the hook. I had settled for being less than I believed I was called to be. I had succumbed to fragmenting my life.

I now know that I am not alone in this kind of coping mechanism. This mechanism can slow the bleeding but does not heal the wound.

In agreement with this lie and frustrated with themselves, people learn to cope with their messy lives by fragmenting. We splice ourselves into different pieces in order to contain the damage or shame or sin. And we end up literally at odds with our own selves. Although this narrative is tired, it keeps happening, so we might as well name it here. Public leaders are constantly battling this, it seems. I can't even keep up with the number of pastors I know who have crashed and burned over sexual misconduct and unchecked power. I'm sure it doesn't begin that way. Actually, I know it doesn't. It starts off as small decisions of compromise and a lack of transparency that is self-justified (I need this), internalized (it's private), and compartmentalized (no one needs to know). Unfortunately, it almost inevitably turns to inward shame and self-loathing, which, to protect ourselves, also turns to forgetting. And rather than helping, it actually worsens the problem, making us feel even more terrible that we are hypocrites and different from what everyone else sees or knows. Keep in mind, your private self-loathing might be more closely related to carbs than to sex, but no matter what the fragmentation is, doesn't this explain so many of our day-to-day realities?

We create narratives to help define us and project public images that suggest we are better than we actually are. Even on the worst days, when our lives are chaotic and we feel stressed, we post a pithy statement to Instagram and caption it "hopeful." Then we feed ourselves a balm of cynicism that says that's how everyone does it, and we segregate those parts of ourselves that get a little too needy or act out a little too much. We are convinced that these are the parts others won't accept and will view as unacceptable (as we all try to hide the things that scare us in ourselves). Ironically, this is actually what separates us from one another, since it's our weaknesses and struggles and vulnerabilities that bring us together.

Eventually and inevitably, the more we give in to a cynical worldview, the more these parts of ourselves become impossible to manage as a whole. Rather than deal honestly with the affair, the pastor simply compartmentalizes it and continues to act out in sexually harmful behavior to soothe himself. The woman distances herself from her marriage because the fear of being honest about her drinking as a coping mechanism keeps her locked inside. The distance she creates leads to more drinking. The porn addict gets lonelier and lonelier in their addiction, all while their addiction to porn grows in increasingly harmful ways. And finally, things can't be contained and the dam bursts. That's usually when people go for help or implode. Like someone once said about being caught, "It was a great grace."

This is what Jenna has discovered that I believe is a *core* conversation that needs to be raised as much as possible.[3] Our only chance at true transformation is through rediscovering our humanity. It's through a recollection of ourselves. A radical welcome of every part of us. A reconciliation at the heart of ourselves. Wholeness.

That's why this matters for the purpose of this book—the study of how we fight against cynicism and despair when they have rooted themselves at our core. The solutions are not in behavioral or cognitive therapy (it's not just what we do or what we think). The solution is in rediscovering who we really are.

In other words: Instead of shaming and hiding, what would happen if we radically welcomed and wholeheartedly embraced ourselves?

This is such a paradigm shift when it comes to dealing with ourselves that you might have to do a lot more follow-up reading and discover the power of it yourself.

This is a huge concept. And some of us can barely conceive of this kind of radical embrace. In his seminal book *Exclusion and Embrace: A Theological Exploration of Identity, Otherness, and Reconciliation*, Miroslav Volf writes from the context of the Croatian-Yugoslavian war as a theologian struggling through what it means to follow the way of Jesus (self-giving love), whose aim is reconciliation. He challenges the problem of exclusion, which frames everything in "us and them" categories that allow violence to thrive, and instead he offers the idea of embrace. *Embrace* is the best word and posture he can find to describe reconciliation and the work of God through Jesus' suffering and death on the cross. He notes there are "two dimensions of the passion of Christ: self-giving love which overcomes human enmity and the creation of space in himself to receive estranged humanity."[4] His work is an incredible look at the real-life implications of how our faith in Jesus and our practice of his ways could bring genuine reconciliation between former enemies. Welcome and embrace. It sounds complicated but might be the simplest truth you will ever hear. Welcome. A radical welcome. And embrace. Volf's book had an impact on me when it first released and I reread it because it was such a foundational theological work. I was struck by how basic it seems that the same principles of reconciliation necessary in our external relationships are the ones required for our internal ones. Welcome. And embrace. It also occurred to me that if we don't know how to practice one, we probably don't have the experience of the other. What I mean to say is, how can we embrace others with welcome and inclusion, as they are, if we have not welcomed ourselves?

I've learned a breath prayer that I use a lot. When I first learned it, I was nursing an injury and instead of my usual running I was trying out yoga. Hot yoga of course, because it needs to be hard and I need to sweat, or I don't consider it a real workout. Anyway, I was lying on the mat trying to be completely still and was practicing this prayer: "be-loved."[5] It's what the Bible uses to describe God's people. The "beloved" of God. The way it was taught to me is that I breathed in the word "be." A deep breath of "be" to counter the other word I usually live by, which is "do." Just be. Relax. Allow God to be with you. You are welcome. As you are. This is no longer about function, but relationship. And then to breathe out the word "loved." Embrace. The catch was that when I breathed out "love" I was to start with my body. It sounds weird, but I did as I was taught. I breathed in to quiet my inner voice that was already crafting a to-do list in the silence. I breathed a deep "be" to remind myself that I am more than what I do. I breathed in "be" as an invitation to God that I was open and available to "be" together. Welcome. And then I breathed out "love." To my body. Love to my sore back and to my aching foot—I breathed love. To my fat middle I breathed love. And this went on. Embrace. And I was amazed. Amazed! In that sweaty moment I had a revelation. First, I realized to my own amazement that I had never treated my body like that before. I was more into the punishing kind of workout. Ashamed of my body. Critiquing and covering and blocking it out. I was disconnected from my own body. And then suddenly I was astounded at how good it felt to be accepted. To be welcomed. To be loved. Be-loved. This is the radical nature of God's ultimate message of freedom. To be loved is his intention for us. Welcome. And embrace.

Consider this passage from Colossians 1:15–20 (MSG):

> We look at this Son and see the God who cannot be seen. We look at this Son and see God's original purpose in everything created. For everything, absolutely everything, above and below, visible and invisible, rank after rank after rank of angels—*everything* got started in him and finds its purpose in him. He was there before any of it came into existence and holds it all together right up to this moment. And when it comes to the church, he organizes and holds it together, like a head does a body.
>
> He was supreme in the beginning and—leading the resurrection parade—he is supreme in the end. From beginning to end he's there, towering far above everything, everyone. So spacious is he, so expansive, that everything of God finds its proper place in him without crowding. Not only that, but all the broken and dislocated pieces of the universe—people and things, animals and atoms—get properly fixed and fit together in vibrant harmonies, all because of his death, his blood that poured down from the cross.

This is a cosmic story of reconciliation. There is so much room in him. So much spacious welcome. God's ultimate welcome and embrace is what liberates us to be ourselves.

Volf explained, "Forgiveness is the boundary between

exclusion and embrace. It heals the wounds that the power-acts of exclusion have inflicted and breaks down the dividing wall of hostility."[6] Anyone who has done emotional work will tell you that a profound level of relief and freedom comes when you forgive others for what they've done to you. And an even deeper level of peace comes when you forgive yourself. Learning to embrace ourselves, all of ourselves, might be the greatest challenge and potentially liberating thing we can do.

As you begin to consider these thoughts I've shared, start by praying this welcoming prayer:

> *Instead of shaming and hiding those parts of myself that I don't like, am ashamed of, am afraid of, or am trying desperately to deny exist—I welcome them. I acknowledge them. I give them a seat at the table. Until all the parts of myself that I have shattered and fragmented in the hope of controlling are in one spot. When we join together we begin the work of healing our core.*

So why do we struggle to accept ourselves? We are convinced we should be better than we actually are.

It is so hard to be you when you are trying to be someone else.

twelve

THE HERCULES MYTH

We are addicted to the Hercules myth. The concept of ascendence is fixed like the North Star in our cultural and personal obsession for better. It's literally killing us. Externally, it's expressed most in the idea of ever-increasing possibilities. You know, the kind that the Enlightenment era of modern civilization birthed—the kind that said bigger is better and there is no stopping us now. Think back to the wide-eyed wonder of every kid and adult as they watched the first moon landing. A day that displayed the nations competing for who could go farther and do more than we had ever imagined. Man could walk on the moon. There was nothing we could not do. And if that's too big for you, then maybe you can relate to the American dream that lives on in Disney films and Hollywood recipes for successful good guy / bad guy plots—where the lines are clear and crisply drawn. The bad guys must be defeated, and the good guys win, propelling humanity's trajectory forward. We will survive. We will thrive. We will succeed.

I get it. I've also had a steady diet of the myth. I would actually argue that it's similar to life in Rome at the height of Caesar's power. Imagine the manifest glory of Rome in marbled floors of palatial estates and colossal statues of heroes and legends. The whispers of a virgin birth and miracle child on the lips of citizens, with hushed tones of reverence and fear. The sweeping, grand Colosseum swelling with crowds singing at the top of their lungs about the glory of Rome—hearing daily the songs that made it so clear that the glory of Rome had never been and would never be matched.

The same song echoes throughout history and among all civilizations. We are destined to greatness. The nations sing it— they hang it on display in shopping malls, which are monuments to the myth: you could look better, be better, feel better, rise to the occasion. Ugly ducklings can be reborn with the help of good hairstylists and cosmetic surgery—they can turn into swans. The rebirth of progress. The endless profits, the ever-growing empires, the militaries that race to the invention of new weapons to display their superhuman strength. Leaders join in the economic boom that is inevitably around the next corner because they are smarter, they are stronger, they are humans but with herculean blood.

You've most likely heard the story of Hercules. He was Zeus's son stuck in human form. He was part god trapped in a regular person's body. I read a self-help book recently that suggests that all of us are like that. That we are trapped like tigers at the zoo. We pace back and forth in the cages that hold us: social conventions, responsibilities, human pain. If we could unleash ourselves from this wretched situation—our containers, our humanness, our limitations, our backgrounds and situations and pain—if we could unleash the roar within us, we could ascend.

Everything inside me wants to believe this. I've been groomed my whole life by watching endless images and stories and everyday people rehearsing this myth in a million different colors and forms and methods, so it rings true in me. Well, at least most of me. But then there is a deeper place in me that knows. My heart knows that Hercules is a myth. Far from someone to emulate, he is a tragic example of living in the wrong direction.

Hercules was stuck. In between. He spent his days and nights proving and pleasing and trying to get somewhere he couldn't go. He wanted to feel like he belonged, but he didn't. And so he tried and tried and tried and faced event after event proving and pleasing and praying that the gods would find him worthy. But even if they did, he would never really be a god. He was trapped in the human condition. He had a body that rooted him to the earth. The dust. To him, his human condition was a curse, but if your heart is open to understand, you'll understand this: to him and all like him, I say welcome.

Welcome to the human race. To the beautiful, tragic "broken hallelujah" that is the human condition—and might just explain why Leonard Cohen's song resonates around the world. Deep within, the song makes sense. Despite the failing, the struggle, the mistakes, still I'll sing "a broken hallelujah." It makes the most sense of all. And before we all despair too much and cue the funeral music and succumb to the inevitability of cynicism and despair, I want to invite you into the real world. I want you to help me celebrate it. The real world. Filled with warts and wounds and weapons and fear and folly and terror and beauty and, well, life. It's not despairing, but it is difficult. It is not pretty, but there is much beauty. It is not perfect, but it does have happy endings sometimes. It's not easy, but it is filled with kindness and goodness and eternal longings and dark adventures. Struggle and intrigue and maddeningly frustrating and surprisingly awesome people with a lot of mundane passing of time.

It is life. And here is what I've learned: If we stop trying to ascend, even for a few minutes, we might just look around and see that this world has much to offer for those of us keen on true adventure. This kind of life isn't lived in fairy tales written in a book by someone hoping life could be different, but by people living out the complexity of being human right where they are—with all the adventures a fairy tale offers, but with all the real life and real self we need.

We need to radically welcome our whole human selves and live in our real lives.

Recently I was at a theater with my husband watching one of the latest Hercules movies, starring Dwayne Johnson (if ever there was a Hercules man, he just might be it). The premise of the movie is that Hercules is not part god but that he started that rumor to get more gigs as a mercenary. He kept up the pretense, however, by hiring a small secret team. When it was time for Hercules to prove his godlike power by doing something no man could do alone, he would enter the scene with his secret team, and together they would defeat whatever monster or army they needed to. Then they would exit the same way they entered, and Hercules would emerge center stage with his sword drawn and covered with the blood of his defeated foe. The people would chant "Hercules!" as his red cape flowed in the wind and his godlike status was ensured.

But in the middle of the movie there was this one scene. It was at the front of the battle and Hercules was fighting along with all the other soldiers of the army he was hired to lead. An enemy soldier managed to cut Hercules's shoulder. It wasn't fatal, however, and Hercules kept fighting. But the captain of Hercules's secret team saw that Hercules has been wounded and made a beeline straight to him. Maneuvering around all the fighting at the front, he rode a horse straight to Hercules, dismounted, and approached Hercules. He looked him straight in the eye, and as he took his red cape in his hand, he covered his wound and whispered, "Never let them see you bleed!"

And that's when it happened. Right in the movie theater, between my fistfuls of buttered popcorn. The screen went black until it filled again with a picture of Jesus. Jesus crucified. Bleeding everywhere. And I started to hear in my heart, *"Nothing but the blood of Jesus can save me."* And suddenly, things started to come together.

We've been taught to lead like Hercules. To pretend. To prove. To ascend. Bigger is better. But Jesus led a completely different way. The opposite way. As Hercules is ascending, Jesus is descending. There is a way we can live this out. In our relationships with one another, we can have the same mindset as Christ Jesus:

> Who, being in very nature God, did not consider equality with God something to be used to his own advantage; rather, he made himself nothing by taking the very nature of a servant, being made in human likeness. And being found in appearance as a man, he humbled himself by becoming obedient to death—even death on a cross! (Philippians 2:5–8)

Kenosis is the Greek word used to describe what Jesus did. He "emptied" himself. It's a word that conjures self-emptying love—the kind of love that is focused outward and embodies solidarity with others. And for years we've considered the cosmic struggle involved in Jesus' decision to leave heaven and come to earth. We've read the text like this: *"Even though Jesus was God."* But Darrell Johnson, a Bible professor from Regent College, explained that it actually says, *"because Jesus was God."*[1] It wasn't in spite of who Jesus was but because of who Jesus was that he became human. Brad Jersak put it like this:

> What if Jesus' humility, meekness, and servant heart were never a departure from God's glory and power, but actually define it and demonstrate it?[2]

Before I really figured that out, I think I mostly felt sorry for Jesus, thinking his humanity was a curse. Like he had to endure becoming a human as an exercise in self debasement. Like he was disgusted by the smell of human flesh. See what a terrible image of humanity I had? This is further evidence that our ideas about humanity are very distorted. Jesus gave no indication in Scripture that he was disgusted by his own humanity. Quite the opposite. This is not what the Bible says—it's what cynicism has taught me about my core and the core of humanity—that we suck. When it comes to Jesus, the very opposite is true—he became human as an expression of love. Hebrews 12:2 tells us that it was for joy that he became a man and endured the cross. And then Scripture tells us that when God speaks about Jesus (the human one), he says he is pleased and is proud of him

(Colossians 1:19). Jesus is not an exception—he is a prototype. He is the first of a new way of being human. And the element that makes this happen? Humility.

But there is still much to say about how cynicism attaches itself to our core.

thirteen

UNCOVERING AUTHENTIC HOPE

I'd like to introduce you to Srdja Popovic. He was a leader in the student resistance movement Otpor, which helped topple Serbian president and dictator Slobodan Milosevic. He runs the Center for Applied Nonviolent Action and Strategies (CANVAS). His book *Blueprint for Revolution* gives the basic strategy and techniques to "galvanize communities, overthrow dictators or simply change the world."[1] Popovic says the first thing necessary to spark change is to overthrow the mentality that says "it can never happen here." Wherever "here" is. Oppression is possible through the spread of inevitable fatalism (read: despair). And anyone that wants to free people from tyranny or even oppression needs to get this very clear: anything is possible (read: hope).

Isn't that refreshing? Reading his book was eye-opening in this regard. There is no possibility of change if you can't accept that anything can change. Including us. A fatalistic worldview is toxic internally and externally. When we think about massive change, we tend to give in to oppression and accept the status quo. This can be political ("We will always be divided") or personal ("I can never be free of my addiction") or relational ("I'll never be in a healthy relationship").

Popovic told about the time he was walking with a group of activists from Egypt who were in Serbia for training, trying to figure out a way to loosen the grip of dictator Hosni Mubarak. He described their pessimism with empathy.

Trying to convince young Egyptian activists that revolution was possible proved difficult. Mohammad, an Egyptian student, expressed his doubt.

"We are all impressed with what happened in Serbia. But Egypt is very different. It can never happen there." We weren't fazed by Mohammad's pessimism. "It can never happen here" is everybody's first reaction, and I told Mohammad that I understood his doubts. The nonviolent activists in Georgia had said the same thing when a bunch of young Serbs met them in Tbilisi just before they brought down their own dictatorship in 2003's Rose Revolution, using Otpor's methods. And I had heard the same concerns raised in the Ukraine before Leonid Kuchma was toppled in the Orange Revolution in 2004, a year later in Lebanon on the eve of the Cedar Revolution, and three years after that in the Maldives, where pro-democracy activists ultimately deposed the country's strongman. All of these revolutions were wildly successful, and all of them started with their organizers arguing that whatever happened in Serbia could never happen in their home countries.[2]

As long as we have unrealistic internal expectations of perfection for ourselves, we will also have warped ideas of ideological change. Radical change—massive shifts—will unfold in our minds like Hollywood productions, not like ordinary human movements. But the truth is that regular, ordinary, flawed human beings have the capacity to make extraordinary differences in the world. This is the beautiful unfolding story of discovering our own humanity. It's not just a begrudging acceptance of our limitations; it's also a celebration of our capacities.

Popovic discovered that the biggest obstacles to getting young activists to dream of changing things was not the hardness of the fight ahead of them, or the big, scary tactics of the dictators and their soldiers' threats; it was their own sense of inadequacy. They did not think they were enough. This is where I really wanted to reach out to Popovic to tell him about the original narrative of freedom in the Scriptures. One of the most incredible discoveries I've made, when it comes to uncovering authentic hope in the possibilities of changing things, is that God intends to use us as we are. *God wants to use you as you are, not in spite of who you are.*

It was in my study of the book of Exodus that I finally put together the image of Israel entering Egypt as shepherds and how the identity of Israel (as a nation) throughout the Scriptures was connected to the shepherd image. It is a fascinating link, all the way to Jesus being described as the Good Shepherd. Israel's identity was connected to shepherding. Israel entered Egypt as shepherds, and because they were honored guests, welcomed by the pharaoh, they were given the best land in all of Egypt for shepherding, Goshen. When we pick up the story in the next chapter, about three hundred years had passed and the

Israelites' situation had changed dramatically. Now they were no longer shepherds. They were bricklayers. And they were living in oppressive conditions. Here entered Moses. Saved from the oppression, welcomed in the palace (the center of power), rising to the top in the perfectly constructed hero myth of all legends everywhere. This was the perfect time for an overthrow. For Moses to rise in power from the center of power to overthrow the power and save the day. This is the herculean recipe for success. This is the stuff movies are made of. This is it. Except it's not. The very opposite happened. Moses failed. Miserably failed. Became an outcast and basically gave up on Israel and Egypt, restarted his life as far away as he could get, and moved on. Story over. Life is hard. Move on. (You know this pattern— the cynical truth, the despairing reality.) The thing is, the story was just getting started.

Moses' exile led him back to something that defined the Israelites when they first entered Egypt. He became a shepherd. Isn't that interesting? The very identity of the first Israelites entering Egypt is what Moses became by default, or at least by descending. And it's there that God spoke to him. It's there that God called and equipped him. Not to be something he was not. Not to fashion himself in the dominant cultural values of empire or violence or wealth or positions of power. No. The exact opposite. To be himself. To be the original version of who he was always supposed to be. A shepherd. It's like God had to wait out Moses until he accepted who he was before he could use him to overthrow oppression. Maybe that's what he is waiting for us to do as well?

Get to ourselves.

To unravel all the disguises of activity and achievement, to wipe off the makeup and pass over the filters until we get to one that looks like the real us. The broken, wrinkled, tired, bad-hair us—the ones we try not to let out but God is waiting to embrace.

I used to think that God used us in spite of who we were. Now I understand much more fully that God uses us *because* of who we are. Once we discover that, we can hope again.

Let's return to Popovic trying to convince the young Egyptian activists that who they were and what they could do would actually make a difference. It might surprise you what he used as inspiration—*Lord of the Rings*. Popovic is a die-hard Tolkien fan. And no wonder. He's been on an epic adventure. He quoted the classic Gandalf inspiration in the movies, "Even the smallest creature can change the course of the future." And then he revealed why that matters so much to people trying to live out hope in real life:

It was clear why the Egyptians felt like nobodies. From a very young age, we are all told that it's the strong and the mighty who make history happen. Newspapers and magazines compete to run profiles of the powerful and the rich, and TV presenters always seem so charmed by the world-shaping elites they interview in their fancy studios. In the West, our culture begins with the *Iliad*—with its scenes of nipples pierced with spears and helmets filled with blood—and continues to this day as a three-thousand-year celebration of violence and heroes and conquest. Think about it: how many movies have you seen about World War II or the Vietnam War? Plenty, I'm sure. But try to count the number of major films that have been made about famous nonviolent struggles. There's *Gandhi*, of course, with Ben

Kingsley; *Milk*, with Sean Penn; plus a few moving tributes to Nelson Mandela. But that's pretty much it.

We revere the warriors, but have the warriors really shaped history? Consider the following: the main outcome of World War I was World War II, and the main outcome of World War II was the Cold War, which in turn gave us Korea, Vietnam, Afghanistan, the war on terror, and so on. But what did the world get from Martin Luther King Jr.? Civil rights and a black president in 2008. And what was the historic legacy of Gandhi? The independence of India and the end of colonialism. And Lech Walesa, the leader of Poland's Solidarity movement during the 1980s, what did he achieve? The end of Communism in Eastern Europe. And who was Lech Walesa? Just an electrician at the Gdansk shipyards, a hobbit if there ever was one.[3]

This is a powerful revelation of the way our dominant narratives are shaped and controlled and passed on through this world. The dominant system works a certain way and controls the narrative. To challenge that narrative means you must be introduced to a story outside of it. That's why the Bible is such a revolutionary book. It tells a different kind of story. It's also extraordinary in that the texts tell the whole truth about the people in the stories. Surely the temptation would have been to gloss over all the fragmented, hypocritical, limiting, frustratingly human parts. I mean, God kept choosing people who got it wrong as often as they got it right. The disciples were a ragtag crew of disunified people stumbling and bumbling their way around—and yet, as they encountered the kingdom, a radical and world-changing movement was born.

That's why the Soviets couldn't stop Tolstoy and Dosto-yevsky from changing a nation's mind. That's why the plays by Shakespeare damaged the elite and the tyranny of monarchs.

That's why the Liberian dictator Charles Taylor couldn't stop praying women from dismantling his oppressive grip.[4]

That's why there is no telling what you might do if you could uncover the authentic hope in who you are.

fourteen

THE SHALOM CENTER

Years ago I spent a few months with a woman who would change my life. It would change the direction of my life at the very least. When I met her, however, I wasn't very impressed. Let me explain.

I had been volunteering with the Salvation Army in Moscow, Russia. I went as a newly saved young person and was content to serve however would help. It was right after the collapse of the Soviet Union and many churches and denominations were flooding back in to reestablish themselves. A generation had prayed for this moment in history.

I did a hodgepodge of small jobs—children's curriculum, young groups, chauffeuring people around, hosting mission groups, running errands—anything that would be of assistance. I knew I was incredibly privileged to be there and to learn from exceptional people in an exceptional time.

I went specifically to help assist a leader I affectionately called Captain America. The reason I call him that is because he was American and he was a captain (see what I did there?).

But another reason I called him that is because he was like a superhero. He was tall and strong and had a chiseled chin. He wore a uniform and spoke with authority, and whenever people were around, it was him they looked to for instructions and commands. He exuded authority. He was in charge. And he was also brilliant in so many ways. He could make things happen, even in a place where it was difficult to do anything. For example, he convinced the American Armed Forces to donate three tons of B-ration soldier food that was left over from the first Gulf War (that they really didn't know what to do with since the war ended so quickly) to us in Moscow to distribute to people who were genuinely hungry and without food. This brokered arrangement included an office in the Kremlin and Boris Yeltsin declaring us the official social services of Moscow. And when I say "us," I'm talking about Captain America and his wife and me. Seriously. It was nuts.

So he was incredible—much like Hercules, it seemed he did things that couldn't possibly be done by a mere human being. The only problem was, he was an absolute jerk. He belittled his wife. He was emotionally abusive and manipulating to people around him. He was emotionally distant with his kids. He was passively aggressive and mean to others. And yet, he could preach and lead and do herculean things—and we were all amazed. But he was also diabolically broken.

He was not who he said he was. At this tender age I decided that is how all leaders are. Broken. They are good and they are bad. This is the human condition. And I guess that's just how we must figure things out. A bit like Machiavelli's prince, I concluded that the end justified the means. That no matter how horrible his personal life was, I couldn't deny that he had done some incredible things. This is just one way that cynicism can enter and cling to our ideals of how we lead and do life.

But then I met *her*. Captain America had to go home for a few months to recover and fundraise for the next phase of expansion, and I was asked to continue with his replacement to help smooth the transition. I agreed. I remember to this day arriving at the tarmac of the Moscow airport to greet her as she descended the steps of the plane fresh from Sweden, the place she had retired after serving for her entire life in various mission fields around the world.

She was old. Small. Bent. Shaky. I was underwhelmed with her presence. She seemed so, well, not enough. I remember her making her way to me and shaking my hand with enthusiasm and kindness. "You must be Danielle; I'm very pleased to meet you," she said, and I said something similar, but in my heart I thought, *Oh man. This is going to be a disaster.*

The very next day was a big one. Captain America had managed, somehow, with his herculean strength, to get us access to a notorious prison in the center of Moscow that no one outside of Russia had been able to get into before. He managed to get hundreds of light bulbs donated for the place, which had been literally in the dark for a long time. And because we were the only ones with access, he brokered a side deal with *Time* magazine and *Newsweek* to come along for the ride.

I picked up the reporters at the same place where all the trucks were waiting and loaded with the supplies we were taking to the prison. They left for the prison, and our next stop was to pick up Commissioner Ingrid Lindberg, the retired Swedish officer I wasn't so sure about.

I picked her up and made the introductions and began some

chitchat about her first night in Moscow. While we were making small talk, we couldn't help but overhear the conversation happening in the back seat. The two American male reporters were relishing the opportunity now presented to them to expose the horrible, infamous Russian penal system and the warden of this facility. They swapped horror stories that they were hoping to confirm and the juicy bits that could highlight their big pieces they'd submit to their editors upon return.

I could tell Ingrid wasn't happy. She turned to me and instructed me to pull the car over. Pull the car over? I was driving on the ring road six-lane highway that circles the circumference of Moscow. Not an easy or normal task. But she was insistent that what she needed to do couldn't wait. My best guess was that she needed a bathroom break but didn't want to say that out loud. What happened next amazed me.

She turned to the reporters sharing the back seat and said, "I couldn't help overhearing your conversation. It occurs to me now that you might not have been properly briefed about our mission today."

The reporters had her full attention. She was even-keeled as she talked, her voice steady and kind and equally assured and strong.

She explained, "Our mission is to bring light to dark places." She went on, "I spoke with the warden this morning and personally assured him that we would be bringing love and support and goodwill and even the presence of God with us. We are honored guests in his house."

Things were quiet now. The words were echoing in the van. The reporters were processing this new information.

And then came the finish: "So you'll need to make a choice

right now. Either you get on board with our mission or you get out of the car."

The words still echo in my ears. I went into full internal panic. I was convinced that in a few short minutes this Swedish retiree had just undone our arrangement with the media in Moscow. I thought for sure the best-laid plans of Captain America had been ruined. I could see the headlines now in *Time* magazine: "The Salvation Army kicked me out on the side of a Moscow highway." It was some of the most uncomfortable seconds of silence I've ever experienced.

And then it happened. These seasoned magazine veterans turned into young boys. Shrinking in size and stature, they stammered to respond.

"Yes, Commissioner," they replied, "of course" and "for sure" emerging from their lips. "We are totally on board with the mission!" they spoke. "We will follow your orders. We choose to stay."

And I could not believe it. What was happening? Ingrid followed up their agreement with some other words that would stay with me forever. My young and baffled mind tried to keep up with her expertise.

"Let's pray."

And pray she did. And as she prayed for God to help us—to fill us with love, to give us eyes and ears to see the sacred people we were about to meet—I felt it. Well, I felt God. The presence of something so powerful and true and good. I felt grace and it made the hairs on my arms stand up, and a feeling of hope and possibility swirled around in my stomach, and my heart fluttered with something like joy. It was otherworldly.

My best hunch is that those reporters felt exactly what I did in that van on the side of the road—because their behavior was like nothing I'd ever witnessed before. They were completely enamored and on board with Commissioner Ingrid Lindberg. They asked her permission for every photograph. Asked her approval for every conversation they would have that day. They didn't take a step without her signaling it was a good idea. The day was glorious and full, and we were all exhausted as we returned to the office late in the evening. And waiting there, in the fax machine, was an article freshly written about the day's events from the young man at *Time*. On the top he had written, "My article, for the commissioner's approval."

What? I was shocked. What happened today? Who was this wrinkled little old woman who commanded such authority?

The next morning, the reporter showed up and said he was leaving Russia to return to the US and wondered if the commissioner might see him before he left. I escorted him into her office.

"Would you pray for me again? Whatever I felt in that van yesterday—I'd like to experience that every day."

And the commissioner did what I saw her do a lot in those few months—she invited that young man into a relationship with God. A good, gracious, loving, kind God who fills us up with himself and restores us to who we were always created to be.

That was only day one with Ingrid. All the days were filled with adventures and daily examples of a power and a confidence and a humility that I had never seen before. She was unapologetic. She refused to succumb to cultural norms like bribery, and at the same time refused to treat anyone (even those expecting a bribe) with anything other than kindness and grace. What was going on? I realized that she was not afraid. She wasn't afraid of anyone or anything, really. She wasn't afraid of losing or appearing small. She wasn't driven to succeed or to keep up with the herculean efforts of Captain America. *She was herself.* She was wholly true to who she was and as a result could also completely trust God to be who he was.

That was the first time I witnessed someone leading from a shalom center. *Shalom* is a Hebrew word that is translated into English as "peace," but it means much more than our English can convey. It's a fullness, a wholeness, an interconnected thriving. It is as Martin Luther King Jr. so beautifully said, "Not merely the absence of tension; it is the presence of justice."[1] A shalom center is leading from your whole core—your truest self. The core of Ingrid's being had been infused with peace. She was patient, long-suffering, hope manifested. And that was the day I stopped longing to be Captain America and aimed instead to be more like an elderly Swedish woman.

fifteen

TRUE HUMILITY

To recover authentic hope, despair must be uprooted out of the center of our lives. This needs to be done regularly, not just once in our lives. Most of us have believed a cynical truth about humility—that it is for doormats and people who can't or won't rise to the occasion. People who walk around apologetic for being talented. But that would be a terribly misguided and cynical view of humility.

True humility is agreeing with God about who you are. That's the best description I've ever heard. And, of course, understanding that God says you are good before any other thing happens to you or through you is essential for using this tool well.

I use a continuum to explain how true humility might be discovered in our lives. I find it's helpful because none of us are ever completely truly humble, but we try. And we keep trying. Moving ourselves into a posture that wants to be humble is a good place to begin.

As we think about true humility as a continuum, let's use

this image to help us. The ends of the continuum are opposites. On one end is insecurity (a constant feeling of not being enough) and on the other is arrogance (a constant feeling that you are better than everyone else). It's important to recognize that if we could use a full-dimensional model for this, the two opposite ends would connect, and we would realize that arrogance is just insecurity turned inside out. But with this model, let's use the opposing ends to help us understand more.

INSECURITY ———————————— **ARROGANCE**

Insecurity is that perpetual feeling that you aren't enough, that you don't have enough (whatever you need: training, experience, courage, education). It immobilizes you from being who you were meant to be. And this happens all the time. People get caught playing smaller than they are, not because they are humble but because they are insecure. This especially plagues people who have been told by external sources that they are less than ideal. Women, people of color, and folks who have been marginalized by mainstream society or by the cultures they are part of tend to lean in this direction. Many of the major characters of the Bible come from this end of the spectrum. That's why they are always suggesting that God picked the wrong person. Imagine that. When we are insecure enough, we will even argue with God. Things like "I couldn't possibly" or "No one will listen to me" or "I'm not good enough" come out of our mouths or into our thoughts when we are living outside of true humility and leaning toward insecurity.

On the other side of the continuum is arrogance. This posture is best described by a story I once heard about

Muhammad Ali. The story goes that he was on an airplane about to take off, and the announcement had been made about everyone having to fasten their seat belts. Muhammad Ali made no movement to fasten his. A few more announcements were played, and nothing changed. Finally, a flight attendant approached him and said sweetly, "Mr. Ali, I'm afraid we can't take off until you do up your seat belt." To which Muhammad Ali responded, "Superman don't need no seat belt!" To which the flight attendant replied, "Superman don't need no airplane either." And the issue was resolved.

You know that place we can slide into where we think we are amazing? Where we are convinced we are God's gift to the world and to the organization at which we work? Where we are the exception to all the rules? Maybe we are too kind to say it out loud, but we believe it anyway. Things like entitlement and celebrity happen here. We say or at least think, "These people have no idea who they have on their team!"

Insecurity and arrogance are two sides of the same coin. And in my experience, they happen when we are out of alignment with our core identity. This can often be related to external circumstances. When we are knocking it out of the park at our jobs or hobbies or life stage, we can slide into arrogance. When we crash and burn at a project or a business or lose a job, we can slide quickly into insecurity. In both of those situations, cynicism attaches itself to our core identity and we hide our own identity issues behind ideas like "people can't be trusted" or "churches are horrible places" or "leaders suck"—when what we really mean is that we suck. In arrogance we are overcompensating for our doubt and fear, and in insecurity we are voicing and giving space to disappointments. Either way, we are being duped by our false selves and we need to spend some time re-posturing our lives to the center—our core identity, who we are, true humility. We need to come back to what God says about us.

How?

I find that visual exercise helps me with this. Take some time now to think about where you tend to lean in your own experience and season. Try to identify *why* you lean in that direction. A character story in the Bible I've often turned to when thinking this through is Gideon. His story is hidden in a crazy book of weird and wacky people God chose to lead Israel during some terrible times. It's chock-full of women, left-handers, runts, crazy people, irreverent and irreligious folks. The book is problematic if you read it as an instruction manual for leadership because, well, most of them end up killing a lot of people in the name of God and that is never the result God is looking for—especially when we read Scripture through the Jesus lens, which is how I believe it's all meant to be read.

So when I use the story of Gideon—or Deborah or Samson, for that matter—I'm not proposing that killing a bunch of Philistines is where we want to land in our own leadership. But what I think worthy of contemplation is what God was demonstrating by choosing the people he did. He deliberately chose people who were not like the others. He chose people the culture or dominant system (religious ways) at the time would have discarded. And God keeps doing this, by the way. It seems to be his pattern. It's like he's trying to tell us something.

When God called Gideon, he happened to be hiding out, trying to keep some food for his family during an enemy occupation. He was the opposite of a warrior in his own behavior and by his own estimation. An angel appeared and said to him (while he was hiding out), "Mighty warrior! The Lord is with you" (Judges 6:12, author paraphrase). Gideon agreed even though he basically said the angel was obviously mistaken about him and about the Lord being with him. I can imagine Gideon gesturing to the distraught and despairing neighborhood and saying, "Where is he then?"

What happened next was a series of events that we don't have time to dismantle, but there are two things I want us to notice.

The first is what I call "the tape." The tape is the internal dialogue we rehearse when we are stuck in our own insecurity. It can sound as diverse as our own experiences and cultures, but the dominant theme is that it is the well-constructed reasoning for why we can't do whatever it is that we are called to do.

Even for Gideon it sounded rehearsed. In response to the angel, he said, "I am the weakest member of the smallest tribe in all of Israel" (Judges 6:15, author paraphrase). In my mind I can hear Gideon learning this as a young boy while being bullied at school by a member of the occupation. I imagine him eating his breakfast and making the declaration that he's tired of living this way and he's about to stand up to the bully once and for all. And someone, his mother maybe, or an older brother, saying, "Ah, Gideon, that's so sweet. But honey, you are the weakest member of the smallest tribe in all of Israel"—and the moment is dismissed. And so is the boy. And then that comment becomes a tape that Gideon plays every time he is stirred to respond to injustice or put up his hand for leadership. And it's that tape that he went to when the angel appeared with a message from God himself.

We all must confront the tape. You cannot heal your core identity with who God says you are if you aren't honest about what you've been telling yourself about who you are.

Getting honest here is important.

This might be a good time to pause. Perhaps now is the time to see a counselor, journal this through, or even talk with a friend about your tape and your identity and how that has been shaping and fueling your cynicism. Perhaps you recognize your inability to trust others or suspect that you are the problem after all—whether you spend your days wishfully thinking the answer is outside of you or pretending you are better than you are. It's time to address the core—that's where change happens.

I believe that Jesus boiled down his teaching to its most essential form in the Beatitudes. There he told everyone the secret to living a truly blessed life—notice that three out of the eight Beatitudes are about getting to the end of yourself.

Poverty of spirit (the end of your rope), mourning (the grief you feel when you come to grips with it), meekness (not trying to fight against it anymore).

All the core teachings of Jesus are the exact opposite of Hercules, the opposite direction of ascension, the end of pretension. We've so misunderstood this over the years of church history and Bible studies that we've considered the Beatitudes wishful thinking—an ideal that we could never maintain and so we should just move on. We've made Jesus the exception instead of the prototype of how humans could be and live with one another. Jesus was a human perfectly filled with the Spirit. And one of the most compelling and curious things about him is the way he was truly humble. He never apologized for who he was. Never did he demean himself or shrink away from his calling. And never did he need a publicity tour. Never did he need position or fame or accomplishment or crowd approval.

So getting to this place—confronting the place where cynicism lodges itself in our lives—is essential to being all that God created us to be. That is the other side of hope. The old board that is hammered into another board doesn't look shiny or perfect, but it holds.

But there is more. Because as much as cynicism roots itself at our core, the story really isn't all about us. It's about so much more. There is another posture shift required.

sixteen

TRUE DEPENDENCY

If true humility is agreeing with God about who you are, then
true dependency is agreeing with God about who he is. And
this, my friends, is key.

So far in this book we've focused on your core identity. This
is because I'm convinced that the original source of cynicism
is found there. So we have been digging deep to confront the
threat at our foundation. But that's only where cynicism is
found. Once we find it in our core identity, we need to get rid
of it and replace it.

True humility is the first step in this course of action. We
agree with God about who we are and then we can disagree
with all those who want us to be something we aren't (including
ourselves). We can stop wishing we were different or wanting
to be someone else. But it's at this place where we will discover
that we still don't have what we need to be who God wants
us to be.

This is where things can get tricky. So many of us have
been fed this part first. We are used to beating ourselves up

and quickly admitting that we aren't good enough. But we're not going to go there.

You are good. That's how you've been made. But *because* we are human, not in spite of our humanness, we need God. This is where Jesus becomes a brother for us in his example. When Jesus became human it required him to access the power of God to fill him with the ability to resist temptation (in the desert) and submit to God's will (in the garden). Jesus, as a human being, accessed the Spirit of God as an example to all of us that we can too. He was almost giddy when he told his disciples that the bad news was he had to physically leave the planet but that the Spirit would be replacing him and filling everyone, everywhere, with the fullness of himself. That meant that these ordinary, very human, very broken, very messed-up people could have access to a power greater than themselves for purposes beyond their own self-actualization. This isn't self-help—this is to serve the purpose of God to redeem everything, everywhere.

So it's not enough to discover our true identity; we also have to discover our true dependency. And this is the final blow to cynicism and the absolute end of despair in our own lives.

Let's consider the continuum of dependency:

SELF-SUFFICIENCY ————————— CODEPENDENCY

Self-sufficiency is when we live in a way that relies completely on our own capacity. Most Western Christians live in this camp. If we are totally honest, we have set up our lives in such a way that we really don't need God. We like him and we are open to him, for sure—but we don't need him. Rarely do we re-posture ourselves in such a way to need God. On the flip side, some of the most powerful people I've ever met on the planet regularly run into their own insufficiency and must access God in order to make ends meet. They are practicing their faith and are much stronger because of it. They agree with God about who he is because they regularly experience his power and provision.

On the other end of this continuum is codependency. This is where a lot of people have incredible ideas that they will never do unless God makes a way for them to do it. "I'd love to care for the poor but can't find a job that will pay me to do it." "I'd love to serve kids, but no one will let me lead the kids' ministry." "I'd love to pray but there is no prayer meeting at my church." You get the idea. It's like they can't do anything without a written invitation, paycheck, or endorsement.

Both extremes are just the two sides of the same coin. Take a moment to think about your own faith journey. Is it characterized by self-sufficiency? Do you go ahead and plan all the details and leave little to no room for God? Or are you waiting for the conditions to be perfect before you will move? Much like our core identity conversation, this one is as deep and as frightening because it leads us to a conversation about faith. It is what we believe about who God is. And this is woven with a cynical thread.

This is where the connection becomes a bit more obvious. What we think about God is deeply connected to what we think about ourselves. If we live our lives with a general belief in God but not any active trust (which, by the way, isn't a bad definition of faith), we are not able to be our true selves. And then the cycle repeats.

What is it that we believe about God? In their book *Reframation*, Alan Hirsch and Mark Nelson invited their audience to rethink their view of God. They repeated the claim that "at the source of all that is wrong with humans is a false and ugly mental image of God."[1] This distortion was introduced in the oldest of stories, the Genesis account of Adam and Eve believing the Serpent's narrative about God. Hirsch and Nelson called it a "reduction" and equate it to idolatry, which is reducing God to something you can understand and control. Maybe like Gideon we are looking around at the obvious difficulty of our circumstances—our messy lives—and genuinely questioning where God is. I think it's a fair question. If we've already been viewing ourselves as not enough, it's not a stretch to understand that we view God through the same lens. God isn't enough, we tell ourselves. And many of our religious sentiments confirm it. God is judgmental and angry or sentimental and anemic. We have been disappointed with God through religion and judgment and cultural norms. And fair enough. We hide from God when we don't know him. We fear what we think about who God is, not God himself. The whole story of the Scriptures is about people misunderstanding God. Think about the crazy things people assumed about God throughout Scripture— killing children and women and one another in the "name of God" until God made a final revelation that spelled it out: He puts his essence and divine nature into human form in the person of Jesus to show us what God is like.

Jesus is the epicenter of the revelation of God. It does not get clearer than that. Jesus. In him is light, life, and love. And there is no fear in love. Perfect love drives out fear (1 John 4:18). We don't have to be afraid of God anymore. He is love. Perfect love.

But we find this so hard to believe. We've remained convinced that God is angry or distant or making a list and checking it twice. Punitive and judgmental, deciding who is in and who is out. Reserving eternal punishment for the parts of humanity who refuse to kowtow to his every command.

That is not the nature of God. To trust that distorted image of God would not be true worship. In an interview with theologian Brad Jersak, I asked him why it's so difficult to lose our image of God as angry. He responded with a revelation he had with his mentor. His mentor was from the Eastern Orthodox tradition, and they were discussing the problems Brad was having with accepting God's radical love. They reviewed together the way Brad used to think about God. "So you believed that God was angry, so angry that he needed to be appeased to stop himself from destroying you? And that this appeasement required the sacrifice of his own Son?" Brad said yes. That's exactly what he had believed about God for his entire life. "I see," said his mentor. "So the problem isn't that you can't receive God's love, it's that you've been worshiping the wrong god. It sounds like you've been worshiping Molech, not Yahweh."[2]

Whoa.

Brad goes on to explain that what Jesus was revealing was the *nature* of God. Jesus was the final sacrifice because God doesn't require sacrifice. He wants relationship. He wants honesty. He wants love. This hit me deeply. I realized the deep, horrible truth that we have received and believed and perpetuated the wrong god. Is it any wonder that we lack power and transformation when we keep sacrificing at the wrong altar? If you want to know God, you can find everything you need to know about him in Jesus. This is what makes Jesus so incredible and timeless and transformational.[3] I remember when this truth hit me deeply. I was listening to a podcast[4] where Brad was explaining some basic theology, unraveling the ways we have portrayed and believed God to be angry and full of wrath and having to be appeased so he doesn't lose it on humanity. And he said it makes complete sense not to trust ourselves to a god like that. Then he broke out the scriptures describing God through the person of Jesus—explaining who Jesus is (1 John 4, for example)—and began to invite listeners to pray that God would open their eyes to truly see Jesus.

Here are his words:

God is love. And he has shown us what that love looks like in someone who revealed God's love as self-giving. He is utterly generous to you—everything he has of himself is yours. He's radically forgiving—there is nothing his blood can't wash. There is not a single thing we have ever done that would hinder him from loving us. And he is co-suffering. He knows your deepest sorrows and your deepest pain. He has experienced it in his body and in his spirit and he's wept blood for you.

That's the kind of love that is extended. And this love lives in you. If you want to experience this love, you simply say, "Okay, I would be willing to surrender myself to that kind of care." If God is really like that, if Jesus has revealed this indwelling Abba who holds us at our worst and in our deepest pain, who has gone into the abyss to find us—could you surrender yourself to his care? Would you even like to taste that love?

So in prayer now, if you could meet God—one-on-one and just look him in the face—where would you meet him? Wherever you'd meet him—open the eyes of your heart to see him—pay attention to how he comes to you . . . open the eyes of your heart to see . . . and he comes to you and says, "I'd like to live here." What is his expression—the true Lord Jesus of Nazareth—his eyes communicate Good News. What's the very first thing he would say to you today? What's the one thing Jesus would like to say to you? Open the ears of your heart to listen. What's he saying to you? We aren't asking anyone to sign up for anything today. *Just open yourself to love.* Would you open your heart to the blessing of God?[5]

And then he blesses people.

I wept. I rewound the podcast and listened again. I wept again. I was weeping at the revelation of God through Jesus. But I was also weeping at the amount of people who don't know God like that. Who have never fully understood the depth of love God has for them. The God of love. The same thing happened when I read *Original Blessing*, particularly the last four chapters that center around the person of Jesus. Danielle Shroyer recounted a conversation in an elevator with a priest. He had asked her a question related to the cross. If we aren't bad at our core, why would Jesus have to die on a cross? Danielle unpacks the reasons in her book, and as I read about God in human flesh—enduring all the fear, shame, exclusion, judgment, and pain the world could throw at him, and choosing forgiveness, modeling self-giving love, revealing the heart of God as open and tender and honest—I wept again. I wept as I realized that I had turned the pinnacle of God's demonstrated love for humanity (the cross) into a payment, a transaction, a functional element of a "law" story instead of the wild thing it is—a love story.

When we know God through the revelation of Jesus, it allows us to trust him. Our cynicism about who he is and where he is and what he wants can loosen its grip from the center of our faith and we can allow his light and life and love to enter. That love can fill our core identity with shalom (peace) and allow us to be filled with hope.

Perhaps you want some steps or some principles or some action points to help. I get it. We are a practical bunch of people. Open Ephesians 3 in your Bible and begin to pray that you might know the love of God—how deep and wide and long and high it is. You will never exhaust it. The love goes on and on and on. You simply need to let yourself be held and filled and loved by that love.

This adjustment on the continuum of true dependency is essential to living from a place of enough. A place of peace. It's essential for moving from pleasing and proving to serving out of love. So if it's that essential, how do we correct our posture to live in the shalom of true humility and true dependency? Answering that question is the key to unraveling cynicism and despair from our lives and then from our relationships.

humility

dependency

Use this graphic to assess where you are and where you might
need to move in order to find the shalom center in your life.

seventeen

IT'S NOT WHAT YOU KNOW—IT'S WHAT YOU PRACTICE

After years of living, cynicism seems inevitable. Carey Nieuwhof, in his book *Didn't See It Coming*, lists cynicism as one of the surprising fights of his life. "Almost invisibly," he explained, "I started to doubt people and suspect people's motives and then my own. I started to expect 'ministry' to be hard and painful—bracing myself for a daily grind and expecting people to disappoint me."[1]

He described leaving the field of law, but before he did, he looked around at the unhappiness of the other highly successful lawyers he met. He felt like ministry would be different, but his cynicism only grew as he interacted with people and they disappointed him.

What if instead of proving and pleasing everyone, we got off the path of ascension and chose to admit the truth about our humanness? What if we allowed our poverty of spirit and mourning to lead us to God? And what if God led us to our shalom center? What if that journey began to transform the way we think about God—moving us from a big, scary, distant, and judgmental God to a loving, open, welcoming, and transforming one? And what if every part of us was welcome in that place? Every part. Every shameful history, every fear, every "not enough," every doubt welcomed to be met with perfect love. And what if perfect love could fill us? What if the perfect love that we are enough—and that we are loved as we are and as we are becoming all that we were created to be—began to overflow out of our lives and into the world?

I think it would change some things.

I had a friend, a colleague, who crashed and burned in his own journey. Leaving his wife and kids and abandoning his faith, one day he just walked out the door and left his entire life behind. I already knew people had issues and everyone is human, but it disturbed me; it scared me. Mostly because we didn't see it coming. A few of our friends met up and debriefed. What had happened? How long had it been going on? Why couldn't we see it? Why didn't we help?

It turned out that he didn't want help, or at least was too proud to admit he needed it or to receive it. Most likely, even if we had offered, we wouldn't have been able to do much since you can't help someone who won't help themselves. But it also turned out that we needed help as well.

At the time, I was struggling and not many people knew. Struggling with my calling and my identity and my own disappointments in people and even in myself. But I kept it to myself. On that day, talking with those friends, I knew that if I continued to lead on externally but limp on internally, it would be a matter of time before I'd also crash and burn. We asked ourselves this question: "Are we still following Jesus?" I know it sounds like a leap, but you've been reading about rooting out cynicism and despair from our foundation in order to be free of it in our day-to-day lives. So it's not much of a stretch at all. The question was less about a crisis of faith and more about intentional practice. We all knew we "followed" Jesus. We believed in him—most of us were "professional" Christians. I regularly told people about Jesus and invited them to follow him from platforms around the world. We weren't asking one another if we believed; we were asking if we followed. And that is a different question. And here is why it matters: if we stop critiquing and start living our faith, cynicism must go.

Practice is the key to stopping the tape and turning off the spectator lens that allows cynicism to thrive. Let me explain. I'm cynical about prayer sometimes. Does it work? Does it matter? Am I the most undisciplined pray-er in the world? And this goes on in my head repeatedly, until I either give in to cynicism and start to believe that no one really practices a life of prayer and even if they do it doesn't matter—or . . . I pray. Cynicism lives in the theoretical distance, keeping me spectating instead of participating, robbing me of the one thing that would actually answer my questions—prayer.

When those questions start arising, I remind myself of who I am and who God is—a posture shift. And then I pray. I use apps or just talk out loud (if I'm alone), and if I'm really into it I use my body as I pray. I kneel or hold up my hands or dance it out. I pray. And do you know what happens when I start praying instead of thinking about praying? Something shifts.

Cynicism leaves me. Cynicism in our own lives and toward other people is dislodged through our actions (a.k.a. practice). This also explains why some of the most hopeful people I've ever met are knee-deep in the muck and the mire of global issues, busy helping others. When I ask my friend who works with refugees how she feels about the future of the world, she'll definitely tell me the limitations and the frustrations and list the statistics (honesty), but she will also tell me of her friend, a refugee, who is living a beautiful life and helping others (hope). This might also explain the long-term behavior that those in recovery offer as the solution for maintaining your sobriety: *helping others*. Seriously. Millions of people have figured out that if you want to keep living a happy, full, and healthy life, you should help others. I think this is because helping others keeps us *present*. Hope is produced in the present tense, not the past or the future. Hope is a beautiful byproduct of faithful practice in the present. An overwhelming amount of our thought life is based on past events or future dread. But our prayer lives? Our real lives? Our serving lives? Our daily lives? That is happening right now. And hope is found right now. That's why our practice (what we do) is essential for cultivating a life of hope.

This is why that same group of friends decided to create a framework to help us "practice" our faith every day. It's very simple, but it has been a game changer at confronting cynicism in my day-to-day life. It is quite literally the other side of my hope—the life behind the painting, a framework for how I live every day.

We decided to match the cynical voice that told us that everyone dries out, burns out, becomes suspicious and resistant to a practice of hope that would foster the exact opposite of that. We remain convinced that the invitation Jesus gives us is to experience life (the eternal kind that never runs out of intensity or endurance) and life to the fullest. We are absolutely convinced that Jesus is inviting everyone, everywhere into more of himself. This can mean that the longer I'm following Jesus the more amazed and loved and known and free I am, inside and out. We resisted the cynical view that atrophy in life is inevitable and embraced the possibility of joy and hope and love. I want to share how we did that.

eighteen

POSTURE

Daily—today, we begin again.

Our faith is not a stagnant set of theological truths that we believe. Our faith is a daily decision to practice the way of Jesus. It's that simple. For far too long we have been preaching a message that faith is a one-time decision that we make with our minds. But one decision is merely the doorway for our whole selves to find faith. A decision is how we open the door to a life. And a life of faith is a lifetime of discovery. The Bible says that when absolutely everything else has faded away, only three things will remain: "faith, hope and love" (1 Corinthians 13:13). This is what I call the trifecta of Christian living. Faith, hope, and love are the holy trinity of responding to and welcoming God to work in and through us.

Unfortunately, we have taken something meant to be beautifully mysterious and complex and boiled it down to a courtroom drama of one decision called "belief." This message of belief seems fine when we hear it because it's so familiar. We've preached it for generations, telling people that if they pray a little prayer and believe it in their hearts, they are saved. Is that what it means to be saved? I'm not suggesting that we are saved by any other thing except the grace of God through faith. But I am suggesting that faith and belief are not synonymous and that we've been co-opted by an intellectual idea of faith instead of a lived-out practice of it. And intellectual ideas of faith, hope, and love are ripe for cynicism to grow and to flourish because they are rooted in an existential idea outside of the here-and-now reality of our own experience. "The cynic is always observing, critiquing, but never engaged, loving, and hoping."[1]

In her book *Daring Greatly*, Brené Brown uses this idea when she talks about who she allows to offer her criticism. She limits it to "those who are in the ring, on the floor—not just spectators."[2] When she says this, she is quoting Teddy Roosevelt, who said:

> It is not the critic who counts; not the man who points out how the strong man stumbles, or where the doer of deeds could have done them better. The credit belongs to the man who is actually in the arena, whose face is marred by dust and sweat and blood; who strives valiantly; who errs, who comes short again and again, because there is no effort without error and shortcoming; but who does actually strive to do the deeds; who knows great enthusiasms, the great devotions; who spends himself in a worthy cause; who at the best knows in the end the triumph of high achievement, and who at the worst, if he fails, at least fails while daring greatly.[3]

Too often, in all our lives, and especially in our spiritual lives, we are spectators and not participants. It's time to get in the ring. I recognize this tendency to spectate in my own life.

I can stand back, looking cynical and critical of mission agencies, for example—citing the amount of money they use for administration or public relations and questioning the impact of aid and whether they are making any difference in the world. But what happens when I get involved in a project that affects real people? What happens when someone I love, whom I'm invested in, is getting an education or life-skills training or now has some food in their house for their children? When that personal impact happens, I'm no longer critiquing—I'm invested. And that changes the way I think about the same agency I used to criticize. That is not to say I won't have important critiques to offer to make things different or better; it's just that they won't be rooted in cynicism and won't lead to me shrugging my shoulders and walking away. They will be rooted in hope and hard work and daily practice. Those are the very things that can change us and others.

We see this distinction in the life of the disciples and the Pharisees. The Pharisees were always critiquing the way of Jesus, not following him. They were filled with reasons and questions and accusations and were forever looking for loopholes and trying to catch Jesus in a heresy. And why? Well, I think the list is long. He threatened their power? Perhaps. They just couldn't get it? Sure. But I think the real reason is that religion, and often religious activity, is a protection mechanism that keeps our truest selves from getting involved. Religion keeps its distance. That might be why Jesus wasn't fond of it. The power that drove Jesus is described in Scripture as compassion, and *compassion* is a word that means to be moved; to get involved. Compassion drives us toward, not away from. This might explain how religion can be so cruel and disconnected. Religion is a barrier to encountering God, and often an obstacle to truly loving others.

Remember those friends I was talking about earlier, the ones who wondered with me about whether we were actually following Jesus? Well, we got together in defiance of cynicism and despair and created something we hoped would protect us from the allure of a distant faith that spectates and criticizes. We call it a way of life, based on the witness of Jesus. Which is to say, a life of love. And we begin each day practicing a posture prayer.

The key word here is *practice*. We don't use the word *believe* because we want an active faith, not a passive one. We also want a faith that affects our whole lives (body, soul, and spirit), not a faith that is compartmentalized as "spiritual." I'm sharing this because it's a very practical and personal way I've rediscovered hope in my daily life. I practice a hopeful posture every day.[4]

POSTURE ONE: SURRENDER

The first part of my daily prayer involves me holding up my hands in an "I give up" posture. As I do that, I pray this prayer:

> *I choose to hold my hands up as a symbol of surrender.*
> *My life is not about me.*
> *I surrender to you, Jesus.*
> *I surrender my preferences—prejudices—and position*
> *to you.*
> *I surrender my fears, finances, friends, and family*
> *to you.*

I take my time.

This is a small but very practical way of getting myself out of the center of the story. And you might be surprised at how helpful this is in cultivating a life of hope. Romans 15:13 tells us that the God of hope will fill us with joy and peace as we trust in him. And that we will overflow with hope by the power of his spirit. The general idea is that we need to connect with a power greater than ourselves to do what seems impossible in this cynical, despairing world. Finding authentic hope will require us to access it from the source. This is a subtle but important shift. You will not find authentic hope without God. God is the source of hope. Hope is an eternal quality. Maybe this explains why the Beatitudes and the Twelve Steps have the same entry: surrender. My life is beyond my control. My life belongs to someone else—someone loving, someone all-powerful, someone trustworthy, someone compassionate, someone who knows me better than I know myself. What happens when I surrender my life to God daily? Relief is the first thing I notice. This life I'm living is no longer up to me. I'm not alone. It's now in God's hands. And the hope that swells in me is not based on the news, or my capacity, or wishful thoughts of positivity. It's all based on God. Surrender will lead us to discover authentic hope because it won't be based on wishful thinking, which is rooted in the future and/or the past; it'll be based on this present moment with our ever-present God.

POSTURE TWO: GENEROSITY

My prayer continues as I hold my hands open and out in front of me ready to receive. And I pray this prayer:

I choose to hold my hands open as a symbol of generosity.
What I have is not mine.
I am only a steward of all that you have given me.
I want to mirror the way that you opened your hand
to us and lavished your love and life upon us.
I want to live an open-handed life in a close-fisted
culture.

It's here where I pause and ask for what I need today. Yes. Today. My daily bread. And I practice receiving what I need. Every morning.

It turns out that an essential part of the eternal life of faith is generosity. Jesus said it best when he sent his disciples out on their first mission: "Freely you have received; freely give" (Matthew 10:8). That was it. He also told them to take nothing else with them. If they need something, ask for it. If someone else needs something, give it. Freely. When I think of generosity these days, I think of breathing. The relationship I have with breath is the same one I can have with God. *Freely I receive . . .* I breathe in. I ask myself, "What do I need today?" The list usually begins with grace and mercy, peace, vision, wisdom—and even though I don't always ask for hope by name, it's what I often receive. Hope. And then I hold everything I have received openly—I breathe out. This reciprocal nature of receiving and giving opens my capacity for more. Not from a deficit of "I need more," but from a place of joyful surprise: "There is *more?*"

Could hope be used lavishly like this? Could hope come as we simply ask and receive? We give hope just as generously as it is given to us. Maybe we are used to finding and holding hope in small sizes, like Gollum with the gold ring in *Lord of the Rings.* We believe in its rarity and it captures us as we hide it and hold it and pet it—"My precious hope." But if we practice generosity, we find hope open and blooming in every field, raining from the skies, growing in every cell, on display in every color and person and place—hope. Freely you have received, now freely give. I used to pray for more strength and power, but these days, as I've started to comprehend God's generous nature, I just pray to be open—open to receive what he has already freely given. Hope is one of those gifts—eternal, endless, and poured out.

POSTURE THREE:
MISSION (OTHERS)

My hands are open now, like I'm welcoming the whole world to an embrace. And I pray,

> *I choose to hold my hands forward as a symbol of mission.*
> *I want to live for something greater than me.*
> *I want to embrace your kingdom come.*
> *I want to embrace and welcome others like you did.*
> *To the lost, last, least, and lonely.*
> *To the poor, powerless, privileged, and persecuted.*
> *To those far away and those closest to me.*
> *Here I am.*

I often refer to this posture as "others focused." "Mission" can sound too loaded with fervor and agenda. But it's when I open my life to others that I discover the best way to live out what I believe. The way to encounter the God of the universe is in the practical, daily work of loving people. Loving others is when I discover authentic hope is not just found inside of me but flows through me as I serve. Have you discovered this yet? When you are serving someone who needs hope, you have it. It's a strange and mysterious thing, but it's been true in my own life. Often, I find it easier to have more hope for others than I do for myself. This mystery is found in the other aspect of the postures we practice: community. The postures are the *what* of my practice, but the people I practice with are the *who*. And this is so important because it's terribly hard to be hopeful alone. It's in connection that hope flows. Even hope has love and faith to dance with for eternity. We hope together.

We don't conjure up hope; it comes flowing into us when we are connected to the God who created it and open to one another. These practices and others like them connect us to God in daily, powerful rhythms.

TOGETHER

Cynicism and despair thrive in isolation. Our current world is the most disconnected it's been in a long time. Ironically, this is happening when technology is connecting us, but our threads of digital connect are shallow. We need depth. Our inability to connect on a deep level with other human beings is robbing us of hope. This is the part of the practice that connects so deeply to all the other pieces of hopeful living. When we are isolated, we think it's up to us to fix it, which is despair-inducing every time. When we are isolated and alone, we think the worst of ourselves and that we are the worst of people. This despair is centered around who we are. Left to our own devices our identity suffers. When we are isolated and alone it's often hard to connect with God. This despair is centered around who God is. Isolated from others who have a different perspective, I can believe God has left me, leading to a spiritual despair.

What I've found as a genuine solution to cultivating a life of hope is *connection*. It's in fewer, deeper friendships that I'm able to be my authentic self and stop projecting what I think others need me to be. It's with other people that I can voice my questions and my sorrows and be heard and seen. It's with others that I can be open to voices that are inclusive and welcoming and loving. As I laugh and cry with people on our journey together, I recover my sense of wonder and awe and joy. Before I know it, I feel hopeful.

Our Infinitum practice only really works if you find some friends to do it with. This is by far the hardest part of the journey, according to the feedback—which is itself fascinating. What people find the most difficult part of practicing their faith is connecting authentically with others. This might be the silver bullet of genuine hope and the hardest thing to do in this culture: authentically connect with one another. Is it any wonder hope is hard to cultivate? How do we create a meaningful group of people who can cultivate hope together? Great question.

nineteen

CULTIVATING CURIOSITY

Did you know that Jesus asked more than three hundred questions in the Gospels (the written accounts of his life in the Bible)? He was asked more than one hundred and answered only three.¹ *Jesus was curious.* I'm convinced that curiosity is one of the best hope cultivators. Cynicism is arrogant. Check it out for yourself. Next time you are cynical about someone, or something, ask yourself what you've already assumed or what you think you know. And then dismiss that arrogance in exchange for humility and curiosity. Ask some questions. Get out of your head. Try to understand instead of judge.

Tell me more.
Would you help me?
I want to understand.
Fascinating.
I'm interested; please explain.

These are a few ways to get started in cultivating some curiosity. Genuinely training yourself to ask questions about other people is a great way to start.

In the practice I do daily and weekly and monthly, we use *questions* to guide us. This is why.

We don't want to live up to some external code of religious behavior—that's been done before. And I'm sure I'm not alone in knowing people that tick all the religious behavior boxes but aren't very nice humans. No, I want to live authentically. I want to get deeper. We've discovered that using prompting questions that help us really think through our motives, actions, and mindsets is the most useful tool. Now, it's not religious; the questions are designed to get us thinking a little deeper about the way we are living and encountering Jesus—they aren't meant to be right or wrong. And the questions also help us to get deeper with one another. Sometimes a question will allow us to share at a new level of transparency and vulnerability. It may be scary, but it's also life-giving to everyone involved.

The questions fit into a rhythm. It's very simple, actually. We designed this intentional practice to be something we could do. Its simplicity is its charm, but it also reveals that we tend to overcomplicate things we'd rather not do. Just because the practice is simple doesn't mean it's easy. It's in the word *practice*. We've found a basic rhythm helpful.

Daily: We pray—we suggest using the posture prayer as a daily habit. It's quite amazing how the daily recitation (especially using my body to pray) can open us to see God inviting us to a daily adventure. We do this daily and on our own.

Weekly: We connect. Sometimes this is a phone call, a coffee catch-up, a Zoom call—whatever it is and however long it is, it's meant to be an intentional connection with another person following Jesus. It includes prayer and questions.

QUESTIONS
FOR
Surrender.

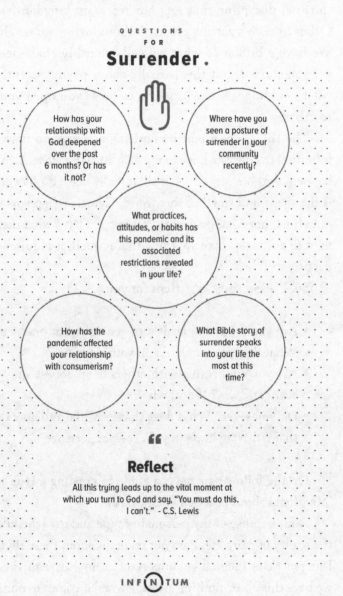

How has your relationship with God deepened over the past 6 months? Or has it not?

Where have you seen a posture of surrender in your community recently?

What practices, attitudes, or habits has this pandemic and its associated restrictions revealed in your life?

How has the pandemic affected your relationship with consumerism?

What Bible story of surrender speaks into your life the most at this time?

"

Reflect

All this trying leads up to the vital moment at which you turn to God and say, "You must do this. I can't." - C.S. Lewis

INF(N)TUM

Above is an example.[2]

Monthly: We serve. Sometimes this is exploring a new spiritual discipline that sets our sights on kingdom values. Other times it's getting practical about loving our neighbors. We have a bunch of what we call "monthly challenges" to get you started, but this is really about paying attention to what God might be inviting you to do as you open your life to others.

The thing you might be noticing as I explain how I use Infinitum to cultivate hope in my daily life is *intention.* Cynicism happens without any effort at all. It really does. It's like dust. It is the shape and smell of this world. Cynicism happens without effort; hope happens with intention. That's what makes it hard to cultivate. Like anything that is good, it requires us to participate.

So, I've got some questions for you:

- Are you following Jesus (not generally but practically)? What does that look like in your daily life?
- Are you connecting with others in an honest and authentic way? If not, why?[3]
- Do you serve? What does that look like and how does that cultivate hope in your own experience?

On the following page is a guide to creating a Hub to get intentional about practicing your faith.

Now, because of my personality type and my schedule and the reality of daily life, I am not religious about these rhythms. I am practicing them. It's so important to emphasize this because we have this all-or-nothing attitude when it comes to our faith.

Hub Conversations.

Create a date to chat with HUB → **Time-bound** the chat

The aim is to **"check-in"** with each other

It's **not** therapy

A **1 hour chat** may look like "Hello"

Catch-up (5 mins)

Jesus, may we follow you more deeply and authentically

Recall the **2 Virtues** → How are we

Loving God?

Loving Others?

Initial Feedback (10 mins)

Focus on one of the 3 Vows, or give specific time to each (30 mins)

Surrender. • **Generosity.** • **Mission.**

(See sample questions)

Time for final input and insights

Comment (5 mins)

Pray (5 mins)

Action points (5 mins)

We have the Hercules myth attached to our own discipleship expectations. We should be praying more, doing more, believing more . . . and we end up in this spiritual state of insecurity and embarrassment—in short, shame. Shame about where we are spiritually is a big reason we don't get anywhere spiritually. Shame and cynicism are the same root. They feed each other to grow despair.

Instead of a cynical attitude about your own spiritual life, keep in mind this is true for new believers and for old ones. Why not simply embrace a practice?

- Pray the daily prayer. Hold your hands up and surrender. Hold them open and receive what you need for today. Keep them open as an intention to share what you have received with others. Open your embrace and your life to others. Be a welcoming presence to others today.
- Pay attention today to how God invites you to live out your intentional prayer. Can you see the divine nudges, the answers, the invitations?
- Invite a friend to join you. There is a free thirty-day challenge on the website you could use as a framework.[4]
- Think through and then *act* on a way of serving others. How might you practice your faith this month?

Make a decision to try daily, weekly, and monthly practices. Embrace healthy rhythms that can move you toward true humility and true dependency every day—to find some peace and wholeness. A shalom center where you are no longer proving or pleasing or striving or shoving but you are at rest.[5] If there is a silver bullet to fight cynicism, it's curiosity. A genuine interest in learning and listening alleviates the spectator posture that allows cynicism to take root. This is true in our quick assessments and judgments we assume about others. We don't take the time to understand their stories or their hearts. In a world of memes, we dismiss them and berate their motives. But a curious spirit will look deeper and ask more. Curiosity suspends judgment and, honestly, we need something to keep the judgment at bay. This is also true of ourselves. I remember being in a therapy session trying to work through some emotional "stuckness" in my own life. My therapist was asking me how I felt about some things and my first thought was always critical. She would ask, "How do you feel about this?" and I would respond, "I think I'm an idiot! Obviously!" or "I'm clearly basic and lacking in fundamental human emotional skills." I was highly critical and judgmental about myself. I will not forget what she said to me. She acknowledged the critical voice: "Okay. That's what your critical voice has to say. I hear that. But is there another voice that might want to speak?"

Is there another voice?

It was in that moment that I realized we do have other options. And we make choices about the voices we listen to— even inside our own minds. The self-critic was the loudest and had the most practice because, honestly, I had not known to quiet it and listen for another. Now I practice this all the time. My old self would have criticized the critic and been stuck in a loop of judgment. "I'm so dumb!" I might mumble to myself. Then I would feel guilt and shame about thinking I'm so dumb. I'd follow that with "Don't be such a dolt—you are not dumb!" But now I simply acknowledge the voice ("Why thank you for sharing, critical self") and ask for another ("Is there another voice that might want to speak?"). This pattern of curiosity has taken root in me now, so that I not only do it with self-evaluation but also with my thoughts about others.

Cultivating curiosity and compassion within us and through us to others is how I process my feelings and thoughts and expose the root of cynicism, flipping despair and finding authentic hope in this world.

"Don't be afraid" is one of the most common conversation starters God has. He uses it everywhere. Even with us. Don't be afraid of God. Of grace. Of the illusive nature of hope. Of the dark. Of the questions (yes, all of them). Of your thoughts. Don't be afraid of people. Even the ones you don't like or don't know or don't understand. Don't be afraid of this world. Or of the immense world inside of you. Don't be afraid to explore, to try, to fail, to learn, to grow, to trust, to know. Don't be afraid to trust yourself to love again. Don't be afraid of honest sorrow and grief. Don't be afraid to feel. To be disappointed and hurt. To die to ideas, dreams, even to physical life. For hope is eternal and it springs eternal. It is furious and wild and growing through every seed of faith and love, planted like a wild garden, germinating even in the darkest places. Hope is with us now, illusive sometimes, shy, but so beautiful to behold. And instead of pulling the trigger to take it home as a prize, we may just find ourselves with enough faith to believe that it should stay right where it is, alive and well, in the wild, where we can keep returning to gaze again and again, renewing our lives with its beauty. Beholding the wonder that is hope.

Flip This Book Over and Find the Other Side of the Story.

This book has been an exploration into some of the deepest and most important areas of our lives. I truly believe that hope is a remedy for what ails us. But the thing I've been sharing in this half of the book is the theory about the other side of hope. And that's important. But where I really learn hope and see hope and have hope is in my interactions with people. I've had the joy of traveling and serving all around the world. I've met many incredible people. And some of the most surprising elements of my life have been *where* I've found authentic hope. It hasn't been through herculean leaders, or seminars, or the deep wells of biblical insights—it's been through real, broken, and beautiful humans. Often those folks I assumed were the most hopeless of all have surprised me with the most hope to give. "Those folks" include me. May these stories renew your hope of humans alive and infused with the glory of God.

NOTES

Chapter 1: Illusive Hope

1. Daniel Asa Rose, "Radical Hope and Laughter: An Interview with Anne Lamott," Literary Hub, November 9, 2018, https://lithub.com/radical-hope-and-laughter-an-interview-with-anne-lamott.

Chapter 2: Cynicism and Despair: The Twin Enemies

1. Markham Heid, "COVID-19's Psychological Toll: Mental Distress Among Americans Has Tripled During the Pandemic Compared to 2018," *TIME*, May 7, 2020, https://time.com/5833619/mental-health-coronavirus.

2. Special Advisory Committee on the Epidemic of Opioid Overdoses, "Opioid- and Stimulant-Related Harms in Canada," Public Health Agency of Canada, last updated December 15, 2021, https://health-infobase.canada.ca/substance-related-harms/opioids-stimulants/.

3. Lilly Shanahan et al., "Does Despair Really Kill? A Roadmap for an Evidence-Based Answer," *American Journal of Public Health* 109 no. 6 (June 2019), 854–58, https://doi.org/10.2105/AJPH.2019.305016.

4. Oxford University Press, s.v. "despair," Lexico.com, accessed February 22, 2022, https://www.lexico.com/en/definition /despair.
5. Shanahan et al., "Does Despair Really Kill?"
6. Shanahan et al., "Does Despair Really Kill?"
7. You can listen to the entire conversation with Sami Awad on my *Mind Blown* podcast.
8. Smadar Cohen-Chen et al., "The Prevalence of Despair in Intractable Conflicts: Direct Messages of Hope and Despair Affect Leftists, but Not Rightists," *Journal of Applied Social Psychology* 50, no. 10 (July 21, 2020): 588–98, https://doi/10 .1111/jasp.12697.

Chapter 3: Under the Floorboards

1. Oxford University Press, s.v. "cynicism," Lexico.com, accessed February 22, 2022, https://www.lexico.com/en/definition /cynicism.
2. Oxford University Press, s.v. "despair," Lexico.com, accessed February 22, 2022, https://www.lexico.com/en/definition /despair.

Chapter 6: How to Respond

1. Styx, "Show Me the Way," by Dennis DeYoung, on *Edge of the Century*, A&M, 1990.
2. This conversation is from an Instagram interview between Scott and Danielle that is available in full form on Danielle's Instagram @daniellejstrickland.
3. Please check out the book *Prophetic Lament: A Call for Justice in Troubled Times* by Soong-Chan Rah (Downers Grove, IL: InterVarsity Press, 2015).

Chapter 7: Our Core

1. George MacDonald, *Warlock o' Glenwarlock* (London: George Routledge & Sons, 1881), chapter 23.

2. Wm. Paul Young, *Lies We Believe About God* (New York: Simon & Schuster, 2017), 29.

3. If you want more on identity and recovery, I suggest reading Aaron White's book *Recovering: From Brokenness and Addiction to Blessedness and Community* (Grand Rapids, MI: Baker Academic, 2020).

4. Check out the book *Original Blessing: Putting Sin in Its Rightful Place* by Danielle Shroyer (Minneapolis: Fortress Press, 2016) and her interview "What Is Our True Nature? w/ Danielle Shroyer," March 18, 2021, in *The Danielle Strickland Podcast*, season 7, episode 9, MP3 audio, 49:47, https://djstrickland .buzzsprout.com/59759/8162041-what-is-our-true-nature-w -danielle-shroyer.

5. N. T. Wright, *Surprised by Hope: Rethinking Heaven, the Resurrection, and the Mission of the Church* (New York: HarperOne, 2008).

6. Young, *Lies We Believe About God*, 29.

Chapter 8: How It Began and How It Ends

1. Danielle Shroyer, *Original Blessing: Putting Sin in Its Rightful Place* (Minneapolis: Fortress Press, 2016), 49.

2. Jonathan Edwards, "Sinners in the Hands of an Angry God," sermon preached at Enfield, UK, July 8, 1741, archived at Blue Letter Bible, accessed February 25, 2022, https://www.blue letterbible.org/Comm/edwards_jonathan/Sermons/Sinners.cfm.

3. See Colossians 1:15; Brian Zahnd, *Sinners in the Hands of a Loving God: The Scandalous Truth of the Very Good News* (New York: Crown Publishing Group, 2017), 13.

4. N. T. Wright, *Simply Good News: Why the Gospel Is News and What Makes It Good* (New York: HarperOne, 2017), 72–73.

5. Wm. Paul Young, *Lies We Believe About God* (Miami: Atria, 2018), 35.

6. Jon Foreman, "All of God's Children," on *The Wonderlands: Sunlight*, Lowercase People, 2015.

7. C. S. Lewis, *The Lion, the Witch and the Wardrobe*, in *The Complete Chronicles of Narnia* (New York: HarperCollins, 1998), 125.

Chapter 9: Who We Are and Who We Aren't

1. Lisa Sharon Harper's *The Very Good Gospel: How Everything Wrong Can Be Made Right* (New York: Waterbrook, 2016) is a fantastic deep dive into Genesis.

2. Alan Hirsch and Mark Nelson, *Reframation: Seeing God, People, and Mission Through Reenchanted Frames* (Cody, WY: 100Movements Publishing, 2019), 58.

3. If you are looking for more on these theological truths, consider reading Brad Jersak's *A More Christlike God: A More Beautiful Gospel* (Pasadena: Plain Truth Ministries, 2015). I also interview Brad about these concepts on my podcast *Mind Blown*.

Chapter 10: Sorrow, Not Defeat

1. Martin Luther King Jr., "We Shall Overcome," speech, Temple Israel of Hollywood, 1965, archived at NPR, "A New Addition to Martin Luther King's Legacy," *Day to Day*, January 15, 2007, MP3 audio, 7:53, https://www.npr.org/templates/story /story.php?storyId=6843464.

2. Dietrich Bonhoeffer, *The Cost of Discipleship*, trans. R. H. Fuller (1959; repr., New York: Touchstone, 1995), 45.

3. Alan Hirsch and Mark Nelson, *Reframation: Seeing God, People, and Mission Through Reenchanted Frames* (Cody, WY: 100Movements Publishing, 2019), 28.

4. Aaron White and I have a course called "The Creative Way Down" that explores the Beatitudes and the spiritual practices that help you descend into the way of Jesus. It combines biblical study with spiritual practices, https://infinitumlife. teachable.com. Also, *Right Side Up* is a free course on the Beatitudes with interviews from people around the globe who have experienced the "blessed life" Jesus referenced, https:// www.daniellestrickland.com/resources.

5. Danielle Strickland, "The Matthew 25 Challenge," World Vision, accessed February 25, 2022, worldvision.org/rightsideup.
6. An interview with Christo is included in a free course called "Right Side Up," available at worldvision.org/rightsideup.

Chapter 11: Ending the War Within

1. "About Jenna," Jenna Riemersma, accessed February 25, 2022, https://jennariemersma.com/about/.
2. You can listen to a full interview with Jenna on the Powershift season of *The Danielle Strickland Podcast* to learn more.
3. Jenna Riemersma, *Altogether You: Experiencing Personal and Spiritual Transformation with Internal Family Systems Therapy* (San Jose: Pivotal Press, 2020). Check out her book and her videos for more information on IFS.
4. Miroslav Volf, *Exclusion and Embrace: A Theological Exploration of Identity, Otherness, and Reconciliation* (Nashville: Abingdon Press, 2010), 127.
5. If you'd like an audio guided version of this, you can find it on the *Infinitum* podcast: https://podcasts.apple.com/us/podcast /infinitum-life/id1155861034.
6. Volf, *Exclusion and Embrace*, 126.

Chapter 12: The Hercules Myth

1. You can listen to the entire conversation with Darrell on my *Mind Blown* season of *The Boundless Podcast with Danielle Strickland*.
2. Brad Jersak, *A More Christlike God: A More Beautiful Gospel* (Pasadena: Plain Truth Ministries, 2015), 3.

Chapter 13: Uncovering Authentic Hope

1. Srdja Popovic, *Blueprint for Revolution: How to Use Rice Pudding, Lego Men, and Other Nonviolent Techniques to Galvanize Communities, Overthrow Dictators, or Simply Change the World* (New York: Random House, 2015).

2. Popovic, *Blueprint for Revolution*, 16.

3. Popovic, *Blueprint for Revolution*, 22.

4. Leymah Gbowee and Carol Mithers, *Mighty Be Our Powers: How Sisterhood, Prayer, and Sex Changed a Nation at War* (New York: Beast Books, 2013).

Chapter 14: The Shalom Center

1. Martin Luther King Jr., *A Martin Luther King Treasury* (Educational Heritage, 1964).

Chapter 16: True Dependency

1. Alan Hirsch and Mark Nelson, *Reframation: Seeing God, People, and Mission Through Reenchanted Frames* (Cody, WY: 100Movements Publishing, 2019), 89.

2. This is from an interview on my podcast in the season called *Mind Blown.*

3. This requires a lot more reading if you struggle with these concepts. I recommend Bradley Jersak, *A More Christlike Way: A More Beautiful Faith* (Pasadena: Plain Truth Ministries, 2019).

4. "Who's In?," August 30, 2019, in *Zeitcast* (podcast), hosted by Jonathan Martin, MP3 audio, 1:14:14, https://podcasts.apple.com/us/podcast/the-zeitcast-with-jonathan-martin/id14748 49938.

5. "Who's In?," Jonathan Martin.

Chapter 17: It's Not What You Know— It's What You Practice

1. Carey Nieuwhof, *Didn't See It Coming: Overcoming the Seven Greatest Challenges That No One Expects and Everyone Experiences* (New York: Waterbrook, 2018).

Chapter 18: Posture

1. Paul Miller, *A Praying Life: Connecting with God in a Distracting World* (Colorado Springs: NavPress, 2017), 65.

2. Brené Brown, *Daring Greatly: How the Courage to Be Vulnerable Transforms the Way We Live, Love, Parent, and Lead* (New York: Avery, 2012), 1.

3. Theodore Roosevelt, "Citizenship in a Republic," speech, Sorbonne, Paris, France, April 23, 1910, transcript at the American Presidency Project, accessed February 25, 2022, https://www.presidency.ucsb.edu/documents/address-the -sorbonne-paris-france-citizenship-republic.

4. You can find free resources at Infinitumlife.com if this is helpful for you to explore more.

Chapter 19: Cultivating Curiosity

1. Martin B. Copenhaver, *Jesus Is the Question: The 307 Questions Jesus Asked and the 3 He Answered* (Nashville: Abingdon Press, 2014).

2. Infinitum Life, "Overview," Infinitum, accessed April 8, 2022, https://infinitumlife.com/overview.

3. There is a guide for starting a hub (small group) at Infinitum life.com.

4. Infinitum Life, "Welcome to Infinitum Practitioners," Infinitum, accessed February 25, 2022, Infinitumlife.com /30daychallenge.

5. If you are looking for a more in-depth study of some of the classic disciplines that you can cultivate, I recommend Rich Villodas, *The Deeply Formed Life: Five Transformative Values to Root Us in the Way of Jesus* (New York: Waterbrook, 2020).

ABOUT THE AUTHOR

D anielle Strickland is an author, speaker, and justice advocate. Her aggressive compassion has served people firsthand in countries all over the world. From establishing justice departments for the Salvation Army to launching initiatives that create new ways to mobilize people toward transformational living. Affectionately called the "ambassador of fun," she is host of *The Boundless Podcast with Danielle Strickland*, cofounder of Infinitum, Amplify Peace, Brave Global, and In My Backyard (IMBY), a Tiny House movement. She founded and directs the Women Speakers Collective. Danielle is married to Stephen and lives in Toronto, Ontario, Canada, with their three sons.